The Jet Age

Robert Jackson

The Jet Age
*True Tales of the Air
Since 1945*

ARTHUR BARKER LIMITED   LONDON
A subsidiary of Weidenfeld (Publishers) Limited

Published in Great Britain by Arthur Barker Limited
91 Clapham High Street, London, SW4 7TA

ISBN 0 213 16778 6

Printed in Great Britain by
Bristol Typesetting Co Ltd,
Barton Manor, St Philips, Bristol

Contents

1 The Blind Pilot

The sudden scream, frantic and desperate, came slicing over the radio like a razor's edge.

'I'm blind! For Christ's sake, help me – I'm blind!'

Lieutenant Howard Thayer heard it, resounding in his headphones, and looked around for its source. At first he could see nothing except the smoke that billowed up from the marshalling yards near Wonsan, in North Korea. Part of that smoke cloud had been created by the explosion of his own bombs, which he had released right on target just a couple of minutes earlier.

It was 18 October 1950. Four months earlier, on 25 June, communist tanks and infantry had stormed across the 38th Parallel, the tenuous dividing line between North and South Korea, achieving almost complete surprise and dislocating the lightly-armed Republic of Korea forces which opposed them. Only rapid intervention by United States Air Force combat squadrons, operating from Japan and from forward airstrips in South Korea, averted a complete disaster.

On 3 July naval aircraft joined the battle, flying from the aircraft carriers HMS *Triumph* and USS *Valley Forge* and carrying out heavy air strikes on communist airfields, supply lines and transport in and around Pyongyang, northwest of Seoul. For the next two months, these two carriers were to bear the brunt of offensive naval air operations. The *Valley Forge*'s flying element, designated Air Group 5, comprised two squadrons, one equipped with Grumman Panther jet fighters and the other with piston-engined Douglas Skyraider attack aircraft. The Korean

War provided both types with their first taste of combat, and they quickly proved their worth. The Skyraider could carry up to 8,000 pounds of bombs and twelve air-to-ground rockets, and the *Valley Forge*'s pilots soon established a reputation for delivering their formidable weapon loads with high accuracy.

Howard Thayer was one of them. He had built up a considerable amount of experience in the four months since the start of the war, had learned exactly where to place his bombs for maximum effect, and, most important of all, had developed a healthy respect for communist anti-aircraft fire. On this October morning, Thayer – together with seven other Skyraiders – had gone in fast and low, dropped his bombs and then got out of the target area just as quickly, climbing and turning to observe results.

The target was an important one, for the marshalling yards formed part of a North Korean rail complex that served the port of Wonsan, on the east coast, where a strong United Nations force was scheduled to make an amphibious landing in support of Allied divisions advancing towards the Yalu River. The North Koreans were now in retreat everywhere, but for the UN pilots who continued to hammer them day after day life was no picnic, for major North Korean targets were stiff with flak.

There was certainly plenty of it today, forming a carpet of black shell-bursts between the target and the unbroken cloud layer, several thousand feet higher up. Thayer was relieved to see the last flight of Skyraiders climbing hard out of the inferno; it seemed they had all made it safely.

It was at that moment he heard the cry for help over the R/T. Scanning the sky, he picked out the other Skyraiders one by one and saw nothing out of the ordinary; no tell-tale signs of fire or smoke that would indicate damage. Suddenly he paused, giving one of the Skyraiders a second, longer scrutiny. The aircraft was in a steep climb, heading straight towards the overcast. Thayer sensed immediately that something was wrong; the pilots had orders to remain beneath the cloud base for the flight back to the carrier.

He pressed his R/T transmit button. 'Plane in trouble, rock your wings,' he called. 'I say again, plane in trouble, rock your wings.'

Up above, Ensign Ken Schechter faintly heard Thayer's urgent call. He was dazed and numb with shock. His last clear memory was of diving towards the target, with the altimeter unwinding through 1,200 feet, and then his whole world disintegrated as an anti-aircraft shell exploded just above the cockpit. The concussion knocked him senseless, but instinctively he had pulled back the stick, bringing the Skyraider out of its dive.

When Schechter came to, his first reaction was one of relief to find himself still alive. Then the relief gave way, literally, to blind panic when he realized that he could no longer see. It was as though he were staring at a vivid red wall, inches in front of his eyes. Something was pounding at the back of his neck, sending fearful shocks up into his skull.

Automatically, he called for help and heard Thayer's response. Weakly, he moved the control column from side to side, dipping the Skyraider's wings. Thayer saw the faint movement, and knew that he had no time to lose. In just a few more moments, the other aircraft would be lost in the cloud.

' Push your nose down!' he called urgently. 'This is Thayer – push your nose over, fast!'

The words registered on Schechter's battered mind. Thayer. There was something about that name. Then he remembered. Howard Thayer was his cabin mate, back on the *Valley Forge*. How the hell, he asked himself, could he have forgotten that?

Suddenly, Ken Schechter knew that he had been close, perilously close, to giving up the battle. The shock he had received, the trauma of hurtling through the sky at 200 mph in an aircraft he could no longer see to fly, had been almost too much for him. Rousing himself with difficulty, he pushed the stick forward and sensed the Skyraider nose out of its climb. He knew, however, that he couldn't go on flying by the seat of his pants, that he had to disregard the sensations transmitted to his body through the vibrating, shell-torn cockpit. From now on, it would be up to Thayer. His friend would have to be his eyes.

Thayer was now flying alongside Schechter's Skyraider, holding position about a hundred feet off its starboard wingtip. He looked across, and felt his stomach turn in horror.

Schechter's cockpit canopy was gone completely, blasted away by the shell. The fuselage was pock-marked with jagged splinter holes. Worse than that, the Skyraider's midnight-blue paintwork around the cockpit was crimson with the pilot's blood. Schechter's face was a crimson mask from which the blood flowed in rivulets, whipping away in the slipstream to dry in dark, ominous patches on the rear fuselage. Thayer saw Schechter suddenly reach up, groping at the top of the windshield, and wondered what he was doing. In fact, Schechter was trying to open the canopy to obtain more air, not knowing that the canopy had already been blasted away and that he had more air than he could handle. He tugged the canopy release several times before he realized what had happened, and that the ear-battering noise that penetrated the cockpit was the roar of the aircraft's big radial engine.

If only he could see! All at once he remembered his canteen, attached to a clip at the side of the cockpit. He located it, pulled it free and wedged it between his knees while he fumbled with the top. He managed to get it off and raised the canteen above his head, tipping it and allowing the water to pour down his face.

For a brief, blissful fraction of a second the red mist parted and a section of the instrument panel swam into view. Then the redness closed in once more, blotting out everything. Somehow, it no longer mattered so much. There was hope, now, that he would not be blind for the rest of his life – if only he could get down in one piece.

Thayer's voice came over the radio again. 'Ken, you've still got your bombs. Drop your bombs, right away.'

Schechter found the bomb release and the missiles fell away from under his wings, curving down to explode on the barren North Korean landscape. The two Skyraiders were now flying southwards, and Thayer was doing some hard thinking. His friend's life depended on the decisions he made during the next few minutes. He knew he could probably steer Schechter over friendly territory, but at the rate the injured pilot was losing blood it could only be a question of time before he passed out, and then no one could help him.

The best idea, he decided, was to head for Wonsan. There

were plenty of Allied warships not far offshore, and if Schechter could bale out close to them he would almost certainly be picked up safely. Thayer told the other pilot where they were heading, but made no mention of baling out.

Schechter, meanwhile, was still trying to bathe his face. The wounded pilot was now, for the first time, becoming aware of pain : a stinging sensation along his right cheek. Raising an exploratory hand, he found that a shell fragment had torn his face from nose to cheekbone, causing a large flap of flesh to hang down. Nausea welled through him, and he almost blacked out. More pain came, in wicked, white-hot flashes that stabbed through his body from groin to throat. He coughed up blood and wanted to be sick. His face felt like a stiffened, aching mask, and when he radioed Thayer he found it almost impossible to speak.

'Get me down, Howie,' he pleaded.

The voice in Thayer's headphones sounded faint and distant, distorted by the blast of air that was roaring into Schechter's cockpit, Thayer, desperately alarmed and sensing what his friend must be going through, strove to keep his own voice calm.

'Roger, Ken. We're coming up to Wonsan now. Stand by to bale out.'

The order brought an instant response from Schechter. 'Negative!' he cried, his voice suddenly stronger, as though the idea of jumping blindly and plunging into the cold, turbulent sea had given him new strength to fight on. 'Negative – I'm not going to jump. Get me down!'

Thayer had to think really fast now. Scanning the horizon, he picked out the dark shapes of a pair of cruisers lying a couple of miles offshore, their hulls shrouded in smoke as they hurled their heavy shells at some unseen communist positions inland. Thayer could see the flash and smoke of the shellbursts, and knew that the Skyraiders were approaching the front line. There was still hope, slender though it might be. About thirty miles south of the line, he remembered, there was a recently-established advanced United Nations airstrip code-named Geronimo. Checking his present position, he quickly worked out a course to steer. Thirty miles wasn't too far. If only Schechter had the strength to hold on, just for a few more minutes, the pair of them might pull off a miracle.

He called up his friend and told him what he intended to do. There was no answer. Alarmed, he radioed again, urgently.

'Ken, this is Thayer. I say again, we'll head for Geronimo. Do you read me?'

The response came at last, very faintly. 'Roger. Get me down. I guess I can't hold on much longer.'

'It's okay, buddy, you'll make it. Hold on now. Turn right. Easy does it. That's nice. We're coming round on to two-two-zero for Geronimo. That's it. Hold her there.'

Thayer watched Schechter's Skyraider waver into a right turn and roll out into unsteady level flight once more, roughly in the right direction. At least Schechter was still responding, which was an encouraging sign. The wounded pilot must still have some reserves of strength left.

Then Thayer glanced over at Schechter's cockpit, and knew at once that the thread of hope was slimmer than he had imagined. He saw Schechter's head fall forward, then rise again only to loll lifelessly on the pilot's shoulder. He realized that Schechter was starting to black out, and that they would never reach Geronimo. They had to get down, quickly, on the first reasonably level patch of ground they sighted.

Thayer looked down. The Skyraiders were flying over an expanse of sodden paddyfields, hardly an ideal area for a forced landing. Then, peering ahead, he saw what appeared to be a firmer area, with one or two buildings dotted nearby. It would have to do.

'Ken,' he called, 'we're going down, right now. Drop your nose and right wing a little.'

Incredibly, Schechter responded and the Skyraider began a slow descent, turning gradually to starboard. As the patch of open ground drew closer, Thayer could hardly believe their good fortune. It was an old airstrip, with a single makeshift runway. During the northward advance of the United Nations forces it had been used by light observation aircraft, and if Thayer's memory served him correctly it could still be used for emergency landings. They were approaching the strip from the east. Just another few degrees, and they would be nicely in line with the runway. Thayer told Schechter to maintain the gentle right turn, ordering him to level out a few moments later when the direction indicator in Thayer's cockpit showed a heading of 270 degrees. Schechter obeyed the order almost instantly and Thayer marvelled at his friend's superb sense of control. Although slowly bleeding to death and only partially conscious, he was flying the Skyraider instinctively, bringing the aircraft towards the strip on an approach that was little short of perfect.

'We're approaching an emergency field, Ken,' Thayer informed him. 'You're looking good. Nose down just a little more, that's it. Left wing down a little. Just a little. Hold her there.'

Thayer looked ahead at the runway. It seemed ridiculously small. Schechter would need to lower full flap in order to land safely. 'Stand by to lower your gear,' Thayer ordered. The reply was immediate.

'To hell with that!'

Thayer knew instantly that Schechter was right. It would be far, far safer to take the Skyraider in on its belly than to try a normal wheels-down landing. In Schechter's blind state, one serious bounce would be enough to turn the Skyraider over on its back, and if that happened it would probably burst into flames.

Thayer took a deep breath. Every word counted now, and every command would have to be obeyed instantly by the other pilot. There would be no time even for Schechter to acknowledge separate orders.

'We're heading straight,' Thayer said. 'Hundred yards to runway. You're fifty feet off the ground. Pull back a little. Easy. Easy. That's good. You're level. You're okay. You're okay. Thirty feet off the ground. You're okay. You're over the runway. Twenty feet. Kill it a little. You're setting down. Okay, okay, okay. Cut!'

In his shattered cockpit, Schechter switched off the engine and sat there for what seemed an age, his hands clasping the control column. Then, with a sudden jolt, the Skyraider hit the ground. The shock wasn't half so bad as the pilot had expected.

The aircraft slid along the strip, trailing a cloud of dust and gravel, and slewed to a stop.

Circling overhead, Thayer saw Schechter struggle out of the cockpit and lean against the ripped fuselage, his face in his hands. A car came racing along the strip and two men got out, running to the wounded pilot. They half carried him to the vehicle, which moved off towards one of the ramshackle buildings on the edge of the field. Only then did Thayer set course for the *Valley Forge*.

He landed on the carrier's broad deck twenty minutes later to a hero's welcome. As he climbed from the cockpit, feeling for the first time the exhaustion from his efforts to save Schechter, he was surrounded by a group of senior officers, all of them eager to shake his hand. They told him that the radio in Air Operations had picked up the transmissions between the two pilots, and the whole ship knew about the drama. Moreover, someone had had the foresight to switch on the transcription machine in the operations room, and the tense jargon that had passed between Schechter and Thayer was on tape.

Desperately tired through nervous tension though he was, Thayer refused to rest until he learned what had happened to his friend. It was some time before the news arrived that Schechter had been transferred by helicopter from the emergency strip to Geronimo, where army doctors patched him up temporarily, removed a considerable number of shell splinters from his face, neck and scalp, and gave him a dose of morphine to relieve the intense pain that now racked him.

From Geronimo, Schechter was flown south to Pusan, where he was rushed aboard a hospital ship in Pusan harbour. There, surgeons operated on him for several hours, removing needle-sharp slivers of metal which had pierced both eyes. For Schechter, it was the start of long months in hospital, first in Japan and then in the United States. Gradually, his left eye improved with treatment until his vision was restored almost to its former level, but his right eye remained permanently damaged, barely capable of distinguishing between light and darkness. Medically discharged from the US Navy, he enrolled at Stanford University, California, and obtained a degree in June 1954 before embarking on a career in economics.

Howard Thayer went on to complete two tours of operations in Korea. He stayed in the Navy and reached the rank of commander.

2 Battle over the Yalu

For the F-86 Sabrejet pilots of the 4th Fighter Interceptor Wing, November 1951 had been a good month. On the eighteenth, they had strafed twelve communist MiG-15 jets which were dispersed on the North Korean airfield of Uiju, south of the Yalu River, destroying at least four of them, and on the twenty-seventh they had shot down four more MiGs in an air battle over the river itself.

Now, on the last day of the month, the Sabres were once more out looking for trouble. That afternoon, thirty-one F-86s of the 4th Wing took off from their base at Kimpo, led by Colonel Benjamin S. Preston, and climbed to 30,000 feet, making a broad sweep south of the Yalu in the Taehwa-do sector. They had been patrolling for only a matter of minutes when they sighted the enemy: twelve twin-engined Tupolev Tu-2 bombers, escorted by sixteen piston-engined La-9 fighters and a similar number of MiG-15s. One of the American pilots, Major Winton W. Marshall, later described what happened during the next few minutes.

We entered the area right on schedule and sighted two large formations of MiG-15 jets coming across the Yalu River high above us. They were apparently out on their own fighter sweep, but they didn't come down on us. We held our formation and turned south in hopes of cutting into them. Just then, Colonel Thyng called out bogies coming across the river dead ahead of us and about 10,000 feet below. He said he was going down to look and instructed me to cover them as the air above was filled with MiGs and there were more coming every minute.

The bogies turned out to be a large formation of Tu-2 bombers and their fighter escort. There were several boxes of bombers in groups of three. They were surrounded by an escort of propeller-driven La-9 fighters. Another formation of MiGs was flying top cover. The Colonel called for a head-on pass by two squadrons of the Sabres. I came over the bombers just as the Sabres struck. It was better than a seat on the fifty-yard line in a football game. As our fighters poured it on, the whole sky became alive with smoke and flame. It was really a sight – our boys scoring hits all over the bombers, and their fighters could do nothing because of the Sabres' superior speed.

Right after the Sabres made their first pass on the bombers Colonel Preston called me and said 'Bones, come on down and get 'em.' We were in a perfect spot for an overhead pass. The entire squadron went over on its back and came in on the bombers from six o'clock high, right on the Mach. As we dove, the remaining bombers turned their guns on us and their fighters nosed towards us in an attempt to turn us from the battle. The whole area was alive with bullets. The bombers that hadn't been hit still held a tight formation and straight course. They were like sitting ducks.

I lined up the bomber on the right side of the last box. My first burst set him afire. As I continued to fire, he fell out of formation and the crew began baling out. Then two La-9s came into my sights and I gave the leader a short burst from my .50-calibers. He seemed to come apart at the seams and dropped like a stone to the ocean.

Our first pass on the Tu-2s was over in a matter of seconds. I glanced to see if my squadron was still with me and then turned into them again for another pass. It gave me a thrill, for this was the first bomber formation I'd ever tangled with. By this time the area was so crowded with fighters I had to weave in and out between them to get in position for another pass. Finally, I squared away on the lead box of bombers and

fired my remaining ammunition into one of them. He started
smoking as my bursts cut into his wings and fuselage . . . I
pulled away.

When the battle ended, the Sabres had destroyed eight Tu-2s,
three La-9s and a MiG-15. It was the biggest air combat success
so far achieved by United Nations pilots in the Korean War.
There was quite a party in the mess at Kimpo that night.

During the first weeks of the Korean War, following the communist attack on the Republic of Korea across the 38th Parallel
in June 1950, United Nations pilots quickly established complete
air superiority over the battlefield. Then, in the afternoon of
1 November, came the first serious challenge. A flight of F-51
Mustang fighters, patrolling the Yalu River, was attacked by six
fast, swept-wing jets that came streaking across the river from
Manchuria. The Americans escaped, but they knew that from
now on they would have to fight hard for mastery of the air.
The enemy aircraft had been identified as Russian-built MiG-15
jet fighters.

The following day, the first Chinese 'volunteer' forces crossed
into North Korea, and air fighting along the Yalu grew in
severity. The United Nations pilots were at a clear disadvantage
in that they were forbidden to cross the river into Chinese territory; this meant that the Chinese fighters could climb to altitude
over Manchuria, dive across the river at high speed, make a fast
attack on any UN aircraft they found, then cross the river to
safety once more.

On 8 November, seventy B-29 bombers droned over North
Korea to attack roads leading to a pair of bridges across the Yalu
near the town of Sinuiju, through which Chinese troops and
tanks were pouring. High above, two flights of Lockheed F-80
Shooting Star jets of the 51st Fighter Interceptor Wing circled
watchfully, their pilots scanning the hostile sky to the north of
the river. The Reds had been up in strength during the past
week, and seven communist Yak-9 fighters had been shot down
in the course of several skirmishes. United Nations pilots had
little to fear from these elderly piston-engined fighters, but with

the MiG-15 it was a different story. Only the day before, F-51 Mustangs operating in the area south of the river had been attacked by MiGs five times, and only the inexperience of the communist jet pilots had prevented a massacre.

Now, as they patrolled at 20,000 feet, the 51st Wing's F-80 pilots knew what frustration felt like as, powerless to intervene, they watched more MiGs taking off from Antung airfield just across the river. Unmolested, six MiGs went into a leisurely climb that took them to 30,000 feet on the Manchurian side of the river; then, in pairs, they came arrowing down towards the F-80s. The latter turned to meet them, a manoeuvre which seemed to confuse the communist pilots, who broke in all directions after making only one wildly inaccurate firing pass.

Five of the MiGs immediately turned away and climbed flat out towards sanctuary on the far side of the river, easily drawing away from the slower F-80s. The sixth, however, went into a shallow dive, and one of the Shooting Star pilots – Lieutenant Russell J. Brown – saw his chance. The F-80 was heavier than the MiG and the distance gradually narrowed between the two aircraft as they plummeted down. The MiG pilot realized his mistake and began to climb, but it was too late. Clinging like a leech to the enemy fighter's tail, Brown held his thumb down on the gun button and loosed off a five-second burst with his .5-inch machine-guns. Pieces flew off the MiG and it went down vertically, burning fiercely and trailing a long banner of white smoke, to explode on the banks of the river. So ended the first jet-versus-jet battle in history.

It rapidly became clear, however, that the Shooting Star was no match for the MiG-15 in the hands of a capable pilot. During the weeks that followed, the MiGs began to prey heavily on the B-29 bombers and reconnaissance aircraft in the Yalu area. It was an alarming situation. The MiG-15 was superior to any of the Allied types it encountered, and for the first time since the war began United Nations air superiority was in jeopardy.

To counter the MiG threat, the Americans rushed the 4th Fighter Interceptor Wing, equipped with North American Sabre jets, to Korea via Japan in December 1950. Armed with six

.5-inch machine-guns, capable of climbing to 48,000 feet and reaching a speed of 680 mph, the swept-wing Sabre was capable of meeting the MiG-15 on equal terms. Moreover, many of the pilots who were to fly it in combat during the next two and a half years had seen action during World War II, and some were 'aces' with several enemy aircraft to their credit. Their collective experience was to have a telling effect on the outcome of the air battles over Korea.

The 4th Wing carried out its first offensive sweep of the war on 17 December, when four Sabres of the 336th Fighter Interceptor Squadron took off from Kimpo and headed north towards the Yalu. A few minutes after entering the combat area at 27,000 feet the Sabre leader, Lieutenant-Colonel Bruce H. Hinton, spotted a flight of four MiG-15s climbing rapidly to intercept. The communist pilots apparently failed to realize that they were dealing with a new and deadly adversary, otherwise they would almost certainly have climbed for altitude on their own side of the Yalu. They realized their mistake only when the Sabres came arrowing down towards them and broke away, diving for the safety of the river. They were too late. Colonel Hinton got a MiG squarely in his sights and fired three four-second bursts. The MiG began to burn and went into a spin, racked by explosions as it fell. The pilot did not bale out. It was the first of 792 MiG-15s which were to be claimed as destroyed by the Sabre pilots before the end of hostilities in 1953.

In January and February 1951, lack of maintenance facilities in Korea compelled the Sabres to be withdrawn to Japan for overhaul, and for several weeks the U N crews in their Mustangs, F-80s and B-29s had a hard time. For the first time in the war the communists were able to establish a measure of air superiority, and they retained it for some time even when the Sabres returned and began operating from Suwon. By this time the Chinese had 75 MiGs based on Antung, and in April large formations of enemy fighters attacked U N bombers striking at targets near the Yalu. Although Sabres provided top cover for the bombers and F-84 Thunderjets acted as close escort, many MiGs succeeded in diving through the Sabre screen on to the bomber formations, where the slower Thunderjets were unable to cope. On 12 April, for example, there was a massive dogfight when fifty MiGs attacked a force of thirty-nine B-29s, escorted by Sabres and F-84s. Three of the big bombers were shot down and six more badly damaged, while the Sabres claimed four MiGs destroyed and six damaged. The Thunderjets, fighting for their lives, scored no kills.

There was more fierce air fighting in May, when UN aircraft struck hard at enemy airfields in North Korea, and these air battles saw the rise of the first air ace of the Korean War. He was Captain James Jabara, a Sabre pilot with the 4th Wing's 334th Squadron. On 7 May, when his own squadron was rotated back to Japan, Jabara stayed on at Suwon to fly and fight with its replacement, the 335th Squadron. By that time his score stood at four MiGs destroyed and he needed just another enemy aircraft to his credit to earn the title of ace.

His chance came on 20 May, when fifty MiGs crossed the Yalu to attack twelve Sabres of the 334th. Two more flights of Sabres, one of which included Jabara, were quickly summoned by radio and hurled themselves into the fray. Jabara soon got on the tail of one of the enemy fighters and saw his bullets scoring strikes on the MiG's wings and fuselage. He followed it down to 10,000 feet and saw the pilot eject. He climbed back to 25,000 feet and within a couple of minutes was fighting it out with a second MiG, which he set on fire. He had time to watch it spin down in flames before being forced to break violently as a third MiG fastened itself to his own tail. He broke away hard and went into a long dive, losing the enemy fighter and returning to base.

Jabara's two victories were made all the more noteworthy by the fact that one of his wing tanks had refused to jettison, a circumstance that would have compelled most pilots to go home immediately. Jabara scored no further victories before the end of his current tour, but he returned to Korea later in the war and increased his score to fifteen, becoming an ace three times over. He had also destroyed three German aircraft during World War II.

In November 1951, the 51st Fighter Interceptor Wing, which had soldiered on valiantly until then with its F-80 Shooting Stars, at last converted to Sabres and joined the 4th Wing in operations along the Yalu. The 51st was commanded by the most celebrated of all the 'old pros' in Korea, Colonel Francis S. Gabreski, who had destroyed twenty-eight German aircraft while flying P-47 Thunderbolts with the 56th Fighter Group of the US 8th Air Force in England. Gabreski went on to down six and a half MiGs over Korea, sharing one of the MiGs with another Second World War ace, Major Bill Whisner.

One of the young pilots under Gabreski's command was Captain Joseph McConnell, Jr. 'Mac' had been a navigator on B-24 bombers during World War II before becoming a fighter pilot. In the cockpit of a Sabre he showed himself to be a highly skilled and determined pilot, stalking the enemy jets day after day. He did not destroy his fifth MiG until February 1953, but by the end of April his score had risen to ten and the following month he shot down six more MiGs, three of them in one day, to become the leading USAF jet ace in Korea with sixteen victories, narrowly beating James Jabara to first place. Sadly, McConnell was killed in a flying accident on 25 August 1954, while testing a new model of the Sabre – the F-86H.

For a time, early in 1953, McConnell was running neck-and-neck with Captain Manuel J. Fernandez of the 4th Fighter Wing, and there was keen rivalry between the two. Fernandez destroyed his fifth and sixth MiGs on 18 February 1953, then shot down four more in March. At the end of April he was actually in the lead, and he held it during May, when his score rose to fourteen and a half enemy aircraft destroyed. Then McConnell forged ahead in a remarkable blaze of glory and Fernandez never had a chance to catch up, for soon afterwards both pilots were relieved of combat duty and sent back to the United States.

Other Sabre pilots, starting their combat careers earlier in the war, might have gone ahead to score more victories than either McConnell, Fernandez or Jabara, had fate not taken a hand. Foremost among them was Major George A. Davis of the 4th

23

Fighter Wing, who shot down three Tupolev Tu-2 bombers and a MiG-15 in the air battle described at the beginning of this chapter. Davis destroyed two more MiGs on 5 December 1951 and claimed another four in a series of air battles which flared up along the Yalu on the thirteenth.

On 10 February 1952, Davis was leading eighteen Sabres on an escort mission to Kunu-Ri when he sighted a large number of contrails north-west of the Yalu, heading in his direction. Leaving the main body of the Sabres to defend the fighter-bombers he immediately sped towards the enemy, accompanied by his wingman, with the intention of breaking up the threat before it had time to develop. The two Sabres encountered twelve MiGs and apparently took them completely by surprise; Davis shot down two of them and was pressing home an attack on a third when his aircraft was hit and crashed into a mountainside. He was later awarded a posthumous Congressional Medal of Honor. His score at the time of his death stood at fourteen enemy aircraft destroyed, a record that was not beaten until the following year. Davis already had seven Japanese aircraft to his credit in World War II.

During the hectic air fighting of early 1953 some Sabre pilots were so keen to run up their scores that they began to pursue MiGs for short distances across the Yalu into Chinese territory, a procedure that was strictly forbidden. On 7 April this kind of over-enthusiasm cost Captain Harold E. Fischer, an ace with ten victories, the chance to go on and become the 51st Wing's top-scoring pilot. In the heat of an air battle he became separated from his wingman, pursued a MiG over the Yalu, was trapped and shot down by more Chinese fighters and taken prisoner.

Of the 792 MiG-15s destroyed by the Sabres during the Korean War, two hundred were accounted for by just twenty pilots, the majority of whom had either German or Japanese aircraft to their credit in the previous war. Some of them were men well into their thirties, far older than the average World War II fighter pilot. Time and again, they proved that in combat at close to the speed of sound, experience and cold, calculating judgement far outweighed all other factors.

Some MiGs, however, were knocked down by pilots flying aircraft which were obsolete in comparison with the high-speed jets. There was a classic example on 9 August 1952, when eight MiG-15s slipped through the Sabre screen to attack piston-engined Sea Fury and Firefly fighter-bombers of the British Fleet Air Arm, operating from the aircraft carrier HMS *Ocean*. Lieutenant Peter Carmichael, flying a Sea Fury of No. 802 Squadron, described the incident.

The encounter that my flight had with the MiGs took place at 0600. My number two, Sub Lt Carl Haines, said 'MiGs five o'clock.' I did not see them at first and my number four, Sub-Lt 'Smoo' Ellis, gave a break. We all turned towards the MiGs. Two went for my numbers three and four, Lt Pete Davies and Sub Lt Ellis. They were seen to get good hits on one, who broke away with smoke coming from him.

Carmichael also got in a good burst at a MiG, which went down and crashed. His report continues :

Though I have been credited with shooting down the first MiG, I feel that it was more of a flight effort than an individual one, because the one that crashed behind me was fired at by all of my flight. My numbers three and four then had another attack on them and got hits on this one. He broke away and the rest of the MiGs broke off the engagement and escorted him away. The impression we got was that these MiG pilots were very inexperienced and did not use their aircraft to any advantage at all. I think it was the next day that we had another engagement with eight MiGs and we were very lucky to get away with it. I reckon they must have sent the instructors down ! These pilots put their aircraft to the best use and we managed to ease our way to some cloud that was about twenty miles away. One MiG got on my tail and my number three fired at him and he broke away. The only MiG who made a mistake was one who made a head-on attack on my numbers three and four and was hit by them and seen to go away with a lot of smoke and flame coming from him.

During these two skirmishes the pilots of 802 Squadron claimed the destruction of two MiG-15s, with three more damaged. To Lieutenant Carmichael fell the honour of becoming the first piston-engined pilot to shoot down an enemy jet in the Korean War. It was a formidable testimony to the Hawker Sea Fury's ruggedness and its excellent dog-fighting characteristics.

At certain periods during the Korean War, notably after June 1951, United Nations pilots noted a marked rise in the efficiency and flying discipline of communist units. The answer, long suspected but not confirmed until after the war, was that the Soviet Air Force had begun to commit some of its fighter regiments to active service in Korea. According to some reports, the Russian contingent was commanded by General Ivan Kozhedub, who had been the top-scoring Soviet fighter pilot during World War II.

From June 1951 onwards, then, Soviet fighter regiments were attached to Chinese air divisions on a rota basis, the Russian markings on their MiGs carefully erased and replaced by Chinese insignia. The Russian MiG pilots showed no hesitation in operating south of the Yalu; carrying underwing fuel tanks, they ranged as far afield as Pyongyang and Chinnampo. For the most part, however, they stayed upstairs at over 25,000 feet, where they enjoyed a slight advantage over the Sabre, and for this reason they seldom interfered seriously with UN fighter-bombers.

The arrival of the Russians coincided with a new set of communist air fighting tactics, including one which the Sabre pilots nicknamed the 'Yo-yo'. A large formation of MiGs would orbit over the battle area at maximum ceiling, breaking off in small sections to make high-speed passes at the UN aircraft below and then zooming up to altitude again. Some of the veteran American pilots observed that the communist tactics seemed strangely familiar, and then they realized that they were exactly the same as those employed by the Luftwaffe's fighters against the big daylight bomber formations over Europe in 1944-5. The Russians had learned a lot in the five years since World War II.

In January 1953 the MiG squadrons entered combat with a vigour they had never displayed before. An improved version of the Russian fighter, the MiG-15bis, had by this time arrived in Manchuria and the Sabre pilots found it a formidable opponent. For the first time, the communist pilots often stayed to fight even though the odds were against them. Many of the MiGs encountered during the air battles of early 1953 bore the plain red star of the Soviet Air Force instead of Chinese insignia.

Then, in May, came a marked change. The 'honchos', as the Americans dubbed the experienced MiG pilots, suddenly disappeared from the skies of Korea. The Red pilots who now faced the United Nations were keen and aggressive enough, but they were inexperienced and they paid for it with their lives. The Sabre pilots who opposed them had orders to seek and destroy; with Allied air superiority now totally assured General Otto P. Weyland, commanding the US Far East Air Forces, 'turned the tigers loose', and in May 1953 they chopped 56 MiGs from the sky for the loss of a solitary F-86. Some of the MiGs were seen to spin into the ground as a result of mishandling during high-speed manoeuvres at low level; other enemy pilots simply ejected as soon as they found a Sabre on their tail.

Many Sabre pilots increased their scores dramatically during these last weeks of the war, with up-and-coming young fighter aces eager to make a name for themselves before hostilities ended. The thirty-ninth and last jet ace in Korea was Major Stephen L. Bettinger, who shot down his fifth MiG on 20 July 1953. He was himself shot down and captured immediately afterwards, and for fear of reprisals the Americans kept his kills secret until he was eventually released in October.

At 1700 hours on 22 July, three Sabres of the 51st Wing led by Lieutenant Sam P. Young were patrolling the Yalu at 35,000 feet when four MiGs swept across their path at right-angles, ahead and below. Young went into a shallow dive, got on the number four MiG's tail and shot it down with a long burst from his point-fives. It was Young's thirty-fourth mission, and the first time he had fired his guns in anger. It was also the last time that Sabre and MiG met in combat over Korea.

3 Supersonic Bale-Out

For 31-year-old George Franklin Smith, Saturday, 26 February 1955 began with a trip to the laundry. It ended with Smith fighting for his life – and assured of a place in aviation history.

George Smith was Inspection Test Pilot with North American Aviation, Inc, a job that involved checking out the combat aircraft that rolled off North American's production lines and ensuring that everything was up to scratch before the jets were dispatched to military units. It had been a tough week, with a lot of flying, so on this Saturday morning, with the luxury of a free weekend ahead of him, Smith allowed himself to lie in until eight-thirty in his Manhattan Beach apartment. Later, over a light breakfast, he wondered what he was going to do with his free time. He was a bachelor, so there was no one but himself to worry about. Well, he decided, there was no hurry. He'd do a few chores first, then make up his mind.

At nine-thirty, he threw his laundry bag into his car and set off to go into town. He dropped off the laundry, picked up some fresh clothing and did a little shopping, and then, on a sudden impulse, decided to drive out to the North American factory at Los Angeles International Airport. He remembered that he had left a test report unfinished the day before, and since the factory was only a five-minute drive from his apartment he thought he might as well complete the paperwork before going home for lunch. That way, he wouldn't have to face the report first thing on Monday morning.

It took him about half-an-hour to finish the report. Afterwards, he thought he would wander over to the pilots' rest-room for a coffee. There he found two of his fellow test pilots, Joe Kinkella and namesake Frank Smith, who were taking a break between flights. There was always someone at work during the weekend, keeping the wheels turning.

George chatted with his colleagues for a while, then they left to take up a pair of F-100 Super Sabre fighters and he thought he might as well go home. He was just about to head back to his car when he was stopped by Bob Gallahue, one of the despatchers whose job it was to supervise the rolling out of new aircraft on to the flight line and turn them over to the company test pilots.

'No. 659 is ready to fly,' Gallahue told Smith. 'Do you feel like taking her up before you go?'

The pilot agreed readily. The flight wouldn't take long – perhaps forty-five minutes at the outside – and it was as good a way as any of filling in the rest of the morning.

No. 659 was a brand new Super Sabre, fresh out of the factory and waiting to make its maiden flight. Smith signed the appropriate technical log sheets and pulled on a life-jacket over his sports shirt and slacks. Because it was only going to be a short trip, he didn't bother with the usual procedure of donning a reinforced nylon flying-suit and boots.

Ten minutes later he was sitting at the end of the long runway, carrying out the pre-take-off checks that by this time were second nature to him. Everything seemed to be in order. The instruments indicated that the big, supersonic fighter's complex systems were working as they should be. Only once, as Smith moved the control column to check its action, did the thought flash through the pilot's mind that something was slightly amiss; the stick felt stiffer than normal. On checking his instruments, however, Smith found that the hydraulic pressures in the control system were well within limits, and the stiffness was so barely perceptible that he decided to ignore it.

He called for take-off clearance, cut in the afterburner as the Super Sabre gathered speed down the runway, and soon the fighter was blasting into the sky under the 16,000-pound thrust of its thundering Pratt and Whitney J57 turbojet. Still climbing,

Smith turned on a course for the usual test area near San Diego, taking the Super Sabre up to 35,000 feet, high above the dense cloud layer that was slowly creeping in over the coast.

Levelling out, Smith began a straight fast run, pushing the fighter up to Mach 1 – the speed of sound. At this altitude the Super Sabre was capable of Mach 1.3, or in layman's terms something in the order of 860 mph.

The needle of the machmeter flickered briefly as it reached and passed the magic ' 1 ', the flicker caused by the sonic shock wave breaking back over the aircraft's flying surfaces and the pitot tube, the stalk-like protuberance that jutted out from the F-100's nose. It was air pressure, rammed into this tube, that governed the function of both airspeed indicator and machmeter. Sound waves travel at roughly twelve miles a minute, so thirty seconds after the fighter nosed past the Mach anyone who happened to be out at sea, within a ten-mile swathe below the hurtling aircraft, would hear a sonic boom.

Trouble struck without warning. Abruptly, the fighter began to nose over. Smith immediately pulled back on the stick, fighting to re-trip the aircraft, but it wouldn't budge. He tried again, using all his strength. It was useless. The dive grew steeper. Still struggling to regain control, Smith called up Los Angeles and reported his predicament. The dive was almost vertical now, and the clouds were leaping up to meet the jet with terrifying speed.

A few miles away, Joe Kinkella was carrying out his own test programme when his attention was caught by Smith's distress call. Looking around, he saw the vapour trail of his friend's Super Sabre spearing downwards toward the cloud layer. Pressing the transmit button, he yelled : 'Bale out, George! Get out of there!'

Smith needed no prompting. With the controls still locked solid and the speed increasing wildly with every passing second, he knew that he had to get out – fast.

He made one last frantic call : 'Controls locked – I'm going straight in.' Then, with his right hand, he pulled up the arm-rest of his seat to jettison the canopy. The perspex hood flew off with a bang and a terrific blast of air raged into the cockpit with a noise like a long, buffeting explosion. Half stunned, his senses numbed by the howling tornado, Smith instinctively crouched forward in his ejection seat, a move that left him in exactly the wrong position for ejection. Even under the most favourable circumstances, in the correct posture with back straight, pilots who eject often suffer from spinal injuries, although these fortunately tend to be of a minor nature. Smith, leaning forward to shield himself against the raging airflow, risked very severe injury indeed. Moreover, in the urgency of the moment he forgot to pull his feet back off the rudder pedals and on to the ejection-seat footrest. Failure to do so could mean the brutal amputation of both legs below the knees when the seat blasted the pilot clear of the cockpit. Later seats were fitted with special leg-restraining garters which automatically pulled the feet back when the ejection sequence was started.

Smith had no recollection of pulling the ejection-seat handle. His last memory was a glimpse of the machmeter, indicating Mach 1.05. The next instant, the roaring supersonic airflow slammed him unconscious as he was hurled clear of the plunging aircraft.

By the time Smith managed to bale out, the Super Sabre was down to less than 7,000 feet, having plummeted down the sky for four and a half miles. Its speed when the pilot ejected was about 1,140 feet per second, nearly 780 mph. Smith had got out just in time. There was a delay of approximately four seconds between the seat and pilot leaving the cockpit and the automatic deployment of the parachute after the seat dropped away; if Smith had hesitated for just two seconds more, he would have hit the sea with his parachute unopened.

Below the cloud layer, Los Angeles businessman Art Berkell, lawyer Mel Simon and Simon's fifteen-year-old son Robert were fishing on the twenty-foot cruiser *Balabes*, anchored off Laguna Beach. It had been a miserable morning, with frequent showers of cold rain, and they had been on the point of packing up and going home several times, but they were keen fishermen and each time they had decided to carry on for just a little longer. Their decision was to save George Smith's life.

There was a sudden, terrific explosion and a great fountain

of water erupted two hundred yards astern, accompanied by a concussion and a surging wave that nearly capsized the little craft. Their first reaction, on seeing the geyser of water, was that they had strayed into a naval gunnery range. Then young Robert gave a shout, pointing, and they saw a parachute drifting down from the clouds, a limp figure dangling beneath it. Quickly, they started the boat's engine and headed for the area where the parachute looked like coming down. As they did so, there was the scream of a turbojet and Joe Kinkella's Super Sabre roared overhead. Kinkella had also spotted the parachute and now radioed the information to the company station, call-sign X-ray Romeo Tango, at Los Angeles. Further away, Frank Smith heard the call and he too streaked towards the scene at top speed.

Smith was in a pitiful state. His clothing was torn to shreds, and his helmet, oxygen mask, shoes and socks had all been torn away by the fearful blast of air. Blood streamed from cuts on his face and feet. Worse still, about a third of his parachute canopy was ripped and useless, and the remainder was only partly deployed.

It was an unexpected puff of wind that saved him. Seconds before he hit the sea, it inflated what was left of his canopy and checked his rapid rate of descent.

Still unconscious, Smith hit the water with a smack. As he was senseless and therefore unable to inflate his life-jacket, he would have sunk quickly had it not been for yet another coincidence : pockets of air were trapped in his torn flying suit and kept him afloat for the minute or so it took the *Balabes* to reach him.

Even now, Smith's amazing luck continued to hold. During World War II, Art Berkell had captained an air-sea rescue launch and had fished no fewer than 275 airmen from the sea. He knew exactly what to do in this kind of emergency. Nevertheless, getting Smith safely aboard the boat was a tough job; the pilot weighed 215 pounds and his clothing was waterlogged, and it needed all their combined strength to haul him over the gunwale.

Berkell knew that they had to get Smith to hospital, and quickly. Apart from his cuts and bruises, the pilot's eyes seemed to be badly damaged. They were horrifying to look at : two brimming pools of red, caused by ruptured blood vessels. While Berkell applied some basic first aid, which contributed greatly to Smith's survival, Mel Simon set course for the coast.

Luckily, two Coast Guard auxiliary cruisers were also at sea off Laguna that morning, practising rescue techniques. The faster of the two, alerted by a radio call, now raced to intercept Simon's boat. Minutes later, the injured pilot was transferred to the cruiser which rushed him to the harbour at Newport Beach, where an ambulance was already standing by to take him to the Hoag Memorial Hospital.

For days, doctors fought to keep Smith alive. His heartbeat was so weak that it was almost unnoticeable, and his blood pressure so low it was off the chart. The doctors were handicapped by the fact that they had never before treated a man blasted into a supersonic wall of air, and they did not know what internal injuries to look for.

In fact, until this moment the belief had been widely held that it was impossible to survive a supersonic bale-out. Only the year before, in October 1954, North American's senior test pilot, George Welch, had been testing a Super Sabre in a supersonic dive when the aircraft broke up at 20,000 feet. Welch baled out, but he was fatally injured and died on the way to hospital.

Now George Smith, in a state of deep shock and fighting for his life, had shown that survival was possible. His recovery, however, was slow, and it was small wonder. Within hours of the accident, his face swelled to the size of a football and turned deep purple in colour. His superficial injuries were much more extensive than had been apparent to the men who rescued him from the water; there were large areas of bruising and laceration on his head, feet, legs, shoulders and back, while his lips, ears and eyelids were bruised and bleeding as a result of fluttering rapidly in the intense airflow. The joints of his knees and arms were loose, too, and as the days went by it was found that his lower intestine and liver had been seriously damaged during the violent buffeting. During the long weeks in hospital, his weight dropped to 150 pounds.

Most of the damage, the doctors calculated, had been caused

by the enormous 'g' forces to which Smith had been subjected. Aviation medicine experts worked out that his body had sustained something in the order of 40 'g' as it decelerated from several hundred miles an hour after ejection, a terrific force that had the effect of increasing his weight to about 8,000 pounds in a fraction of a second. The weight of every organ in his body had increased correspondingly and his super-heavy blood had caused severe haemorrhage as it pounded around his body. Adding to the overall damage was the fact that Smith had tumbled uncontrollably between leaving his seat and his parachute deploying, with consequent rapid fluctuations in the 'g' forces he was experiencing and further severe strain on his internal organs.

While Smith was fighting his way back towards recovery, Navy salvage teams were searching for the remains of his Super Sabre. They eventually located it less than a mile offshore, in 134 feet of water. In over a month of salvage operations they succeeded in recovering ninety per cent of the aircraft : tiny fragments of metal that filled fifty barrels. The largest chunk pulled up was the compressed, impacted engine. For weeks, engineers pored over the wreckage in a hangar at the North American factory, and finally came up with the theory that the failure of a coupling in the hydraulic system had been at the root of the trouble. Modifications were carried out on all other F-100s; George Smith's traumatic experience had not been in vain.

Smith lay in hospital for seven months while doctors and aviation medicine experts kept him under constant observation. On 23 August 1955 he was once again pronounced physically fit and regained his commercial flying certificate, returning to his old job with North American. His weight increased again, but only as far as 175 pounds. He actually felt a lot fitter for the weight loss, but as he was fond of remarking to people who asked him about his supersonic escape : 'It sure is one hell of a way to slim!'

By an odd coincidence, a few days before Smith regained his commercial licence a second pilot made a successful supersonic escape on the other side of the Atlantic. He was 22 year-old Flying Officer Hedley Molland, a fighter pilot with No. 263 Squadron, Royal Air Force. Based at Wattisham, in Suffolk, No. 263 had recently exchanged its aging Gloster Meteors for modern swept-wing Hawker Hunter fighters, which were capable of exceeding Mach 1 in a shallow dive.

Just after noon on 3 August 1955, Molland and a sergeant pilot named Alan Blow took off in their Hunters and climbed out over the sea. For the next fifteen minutes the two pilots carried out practice interceptions on each other, filming the results with their camera guns. Then, with Molland tail-chasing Blow's Hunter, they went up to 40,000 feet, where they flew straight and level for a minute before entering a shallow dive.

A few seconds later, the two fighters slipped gently past Mach 1, still over the sea about four miles off Felixstowe. Suddenly, Molland noticed that he was gradually overhauling Blow's aircraft, so he eased back the stick to check the dive. At that speed the controls should have been fairly stiff, so Molland was surprised when the stick moved back easily. He was even more surprised, not to say alarmed, when nothing happened; the Hunter continued to dive, the angle growing steeper all the time.

At 30,000 feet, Molland decided to bale out, although not without some misgivings. A glance at the machmeter showed that it was reading 1.1. Molland had heard about George Smith, and knew something of the injuries the American had sustained. With this in mind, it looked as though his own chances of survival were pretty slim, yet it was better to take the chance than to sit in the cockpit and wait for certain death.

Despite his dire peril, Molland's brain stayed calm. His one main fear was that if he jettisoned the cockpit canopy, the sudden inrush of air would prevent him reaching up to pull down the handle of his ejection seat, so he decided to carry out both actions simultaneously. Gripping the firing handle with his left hand, he pulled the hood jettison handle with his right. The cockpit canopy flew off and the airflow roared in with a noise like an express train, blinding him. He couldn't see anything, but he had managed to keep his grip on the seat firing handle and now he pulled it, bringing the protective blind down over his face and igniting the ejection cartridge.

Molland blacked out as soon as he was blasted into the airflow. He was unconscious only for a few seconds, and when he came to he found himself falling in his seat with the air whistling past him. His Martin-Baker ejection seat was fitted with two drogue parachutes; both had deployed successfully and the seat, with Molland still strapped in it, was falling in an upright position and decelerating gradually. A few months earlier, George Smith's injuries would probably have been fewer if he had enjoyed the benefit of a similar seat but his Super Sabre was fitted with an American seat which was not equipped with drogues, and consequently tumbled wildly.

Molland had baled out at an altitude of about 25,000 feet. With an indicated Mach number of 1.1, that meant he had ejected at a true airspeed of around 760 mph. In getting out at 25,000 feet he was a lot more fortunate than Smith, for the atmosphere at that altitude was far less dense and its 'brick wall' effect on his hurtling body much less damaging.

As he dropped seawards in his seat, Molland was relieved to discover that he could see again. Then, with a sudden shock, he realized that his left arm seemed to have disappeared. Groping frantically for it, he found that it had been caught by the airflow and dragged round the back of the seat with such force that the bone had broken between shoulder and elbow. He hauled it in with his right hand and tucked it into the seat straps to keep it out of the way. Almost dispassionately, he noticed that his wristwatch had been torn off by the blast, as had his oxygen mask, flying helmet, left shoe and sock. If he had baled out a few thousand feet higher up, he might have perished from oxygen starvation. His face was painful, and he discovered later that one of his straps had lashed him fiercely, blackening both his eyes and making his nose bleed. Also, he saw that the attachments which held his dinghy to his Mae West lifejacket had come undone.

He reached down and managed to refasten one of the dinghy attachments. As he did so, he saw a splash far below him as his

Hunter plunged into the sea. Then, as he passed through 10,000 feet, his seat fell away cleanly and his parachute opened.

He was about three miles offshore, but the wind was carrying him out to sea all the time and he remembered with a sudden shock that he couldn't swim. He would have to rely on his Mae West and dinghy, and as the sea drew nearer he inflated the life-jacket as a precautionary measure. He hit the water a few minutes later and at once found himself in trouble when he became entangled with his parachute shroud lines. He tried to inflate his dinghy, but with only one hand was unable to manage it. His lifejacket kept him on the surface, but he spent an uncomfortable few minutes being dragged along by the billowing canopy, which refused to collapse.

As things turned out, it was the canopy which attracted the attention of the crew of a tug, cruising a few hundred yards away, and guided the vessel to the spot. Molland was picked up within ten minutes and the tug took him to Ipswich, where he was transferred to the Borough General Hospital. Doctors told him that he had a fractured pelvis in addition to his broken arm, but apart from that his injuries were not serious.

Molland had been lucky. Just how lucky, he learned from the tug's crew, who told him cheerfully that they had been pulling a target to provide firing practice for some shore batteries. If the pilot had baled out a couple of minutes earlier, he would have landed amid a barrage of shells.

4 Eject!

Her name was *Ark Royal*, and she was the mightiest of the Royal Navy's warships. With a displacement of 43,000 tons and a length of 720 feet, she was small by comparison with America's latest aircraft carriers, but she carried a potent force of thirty strike aircraft and six anti-submarine helicopters. Since her commissioning in 1955 she had served Britain's interests well in many parts of the world. Soon she would be withdrawn for a complete refit, extending her useful life into the late 1970s as the last of Britain's fleet carriers; first, however, she had a vital operational task to perform.

In May 1966, HMS *Ark Royal* was diverted to the east coast of Africa to take part in what was known as the 'oil watch', patrolling the seas off the port of Beira to intercept any tankers carrying oil for the rebel régime in Rhodesia, which had made its unilateral declaration of independence the previous November. It was an exacting task, for the area to be searched was twice the size of the British Isles. *Ark Royal*'s predecessor on the 'oil watch', HMS *Eagle*, had been on station off Beira for seventy-one days, her aircraft flying over a thousand sorties in that time and her helicopters a further thousand.

The oil-watch flying was not without its risks. The carrier was the only base in the area; there was no diversion airfield available in the event of an emergency. With flying going on at a fairly intense rate, the occasional emergency was inevitable – such as that which faced Lieutenant Allan Tarver, a Sea Vixen pilot with *Ark Royal*'s No. 890 Squadron, on the morning of 10 May 1966.

Tarver was heading back to the carrier at the end of a patrol when several things happened all at once. The port engine flamed out, the electrical system packed in completely, and the instruments indicated that fuel was escaping from the Vixen's tanks at an alarming rate. Tarver immediately called up the *Ark Royal*, and was advised that a Scimitar tanker aircraft had just been catapulted off and was on its way to rendezvous with the Vixen, which by this time had begun to lose height steadily.

At 15,000 feet, with the *Ark* still forty miles away, Tarver spotted the Scimitar approaching from ten o'clock. The Scimitar pilot, Lieutenant Robin Munro-Davies, manoeuvred his aircraft into position above and ahead of the Vixen; from the latter's cockpit, Tarver saw the drogue stream towards him from the tanker. Five times, he tried to make contact with the Vixen's refuelling probe, but by now the heavy aircraft had become unstable and unwieldy and it was impossible to keep it steady enough. Suddenly, the whine of the Vixen's one remaining engine died away as the fuel tanks ran dry and the aircraft started to go down rapidly. The pilot could now see the carrier on the horizon; there was no hope of reaching her, but at least he could try and stretch the glide for as long as possible before he and his observer, Lieutenant John Stutchbury, were forced to eject. The closer they were to the *Ark Royal*, the better their chances of being picked up quickly.

The de Havilland Sea Vixen, however, was not designed to glide. Powered by two Rolls-Royce Avon turbojets, spanning 51 feet and with a length of over 55 feet, its loaded weight was 37,000 pounds and it was designed to strike hard and fast at speeds of over 600 miles an hour. The Vixen, in fact, glided like a brick.

At 6,000 feet, Tarver ordered his observer to eject. Out of the corner of his eye he saw Stutchbury reach up, grasp the firing handle of his ejection seat, and jerk the blind down over his face.

Nothing happened. Over the intercom, Tarver yelled at the observer to try and bale out manually while he held the aircraft as steady as possible. It was not as easy as it sounded; the observer in a Sea Vixen had a pretty uncomfortable position, his seat buried in the starboard side of the fuselage so that his head was just about level with the pilot's backside. It was a tight enough squeeze for the average man : but for John Stutchbury, six feet tall with unusually broad shoulders, it was dreadfully cramped. There was no cockpit canopy over the observer, just a hatch in the top of the fuselage; this should have blasted clear when he pulled the handle – but it hadn't.

Stutchbury now pushed the hatch aside and through the perspex of the canopy Tarver saw it whirl away in the slipstream. A second later, Stutchbury's head and shoulders emerged – and stuck fast in the opening. By this time the Vixen was down to 3,000 feet. Tarver shoved the stick hard over, praying that Stutchbury would fall clear as the aircraft rolled over on her back, but the observer still hung there, buffeted by the 200-knot slipstream. Again Tarver rolled the aircraft, still with no effect. There was just one more chance : he lowered the flaps, reducing the airspeed to 130 knots. The force of the airflow was much less now, and this might just enable the observer to struggle clear. For an instant, it looked as though the plan would work; more of Stutchbury's body slid through the hatch until the observer was lying flat along the top of the fuselage, but something still seemed to be holding him in the cockpit. Tarver leaned over into the observer's compartment, his hand groping for Stutchbury's feet. With all his strength, he fought to push his friend clear. It was no use; the observer now seemed to be unconscious.

There was nothing more that Tarver could do. Even if Stutchbury got clear of the aircraft now, his parachute would not have time to open. The altimeter showed 400 feet and the Vixen was wallowing on the edge of a stall.

Circling overhead in his Scimitar, Lieutenant Munro-Davies saw Tarver's Vixen enter a sudden roll to port. When the aircraft was at about sixty degrees, a black shape hurtled from the cockpit : the pilot's ejection seat. That was all Munro-Davies saw before the whole scene dissolved in a fountain of spray as the Vixen hit the water. The Scimitar pilot reported that Tarver could not possibly have survived.

But Tarver was still very much alive. His parachute had only

partially deployed and he had been stunned by the impact when
he hit the sea, but he was able to claw his way from under the
silken folds of the canopy and inflate his rubber life-raft. Twenty
minutes later, he was picked up by a Wessex helicopter from the
Ark Royal. His only injury was a strained muscle in his back.
For his courage in staying with the aircraft to try and save his
friend's life, almost sacrificing his own chance of survival in so
doing, he was later awarded the George Medal.

Ejection seats were first used by the German Luftwaffe during
World War II, and by the early 1950s they were standard equipment in most high-performance aircraft. In some multi-seat
combat types designed since 1945, however, only the pilot (or
pilots) have had the benefit of ejection seats, other crew members having to abandon the aircraft by conventional means in an
emergency. This fact was not so important in the days when
bomber aircraft were designed to penetrate enemy defences at
high level, because it gave the pilot time to retain control while
the rest of his crew jumped before he saved himself, but in the
early 1960s low-level operations became the only means of getting through hostile radar and missile defences, and crew members suddenly found themselves with only seconds in which to get
out of a crippled aircraft. This means, simply, that there have
been circumstances when a pilot has been unable to climb high
enough for other crew members to bale out with any real hope
of survival, or to make a controlled crash landing. Under those
circumstances, pilots have had to make one of the most terrible
of all decisions: whether to eject and save themselves or to die
with the rest of the crew. Some have taken the latter course,
although logically the pilot should save himself, for by the time
he decides to eject there is usually no hope for the other crew
members.

Sometimes, however, quick thinking and instant reactions have
saved a potentially disastrous situation. One such occasion was
in 1967, when Flight Lieutenant Godfrey Ledwidge and his
navigator, Flight Lieutenant John Steward, were flying a
Canberra jet bomber on a training mission from their RAF base

in West Germany. They had completed a practice bombing run and were returning home at 500 feet when they suddenly encountered serious trouble.

Ledwidge turned right, in response to a course correction from his navigator, then moved the control column to bring the Canberra back to level flight again. Nothing happened: the ailerons were jammed solid at an angle of about thirty degrees.

Over the intercom, Steward heard the pilot's warning shout: 'Stand by for some " g ".' Thinking that they were taking evasive action to avoid another aircraft, for the low-level air space over West Germany is heavily congested by military training flights, Steward braced himself. Then Ledwidge called again, breathlessly: 'Stand by for a lot of negative " g ". I think we've lost an aileron!'

The seating in this particular mark of Canberra was rather similar to that of the naval Sea Vixen described earlier in this chapter, with the pilot seated under a transparent cockpit canopy raised above the port side of the nose and his navigator buried in the fuselage beside him, his head level with the pilot's knees. In the Canberra, however, the navigator had no ejection seat; in an emergency, he had to make his exit through a hatch in the fuselage side. When this was jettisoned, a windbreak popped out, shielding him from the airflow as he jumped.

Ledwidge knew at once that Steward would have no hope of getting out at this height, so he applied full power and hauled back the control column in a desperate attempt to gain a few thousand feet. The Canberra immediately entered a roll, which the pilot managed to slow down by using the rudder and juggling with the power of the engine, but he was unable to prevent the aircraft going over on its back. As it went upside down the nose dropped, so Ledwidge pushed the control column hard forward and speeded up the roll by again using the rudder.

The nose began to come up agonizingly slowly, and Ledwidge now eased the control column fully back. Beneath them, the ground flashed by only feet away; if the pilot had not speeded up the roll he and his navigator would now be dead, the Canberra a mass of scattered wreckage.

Still rolling, with the pilot applying full rudder one way or the other to speed up or slow down the rate of roll, the Canberra gyrated up to 8,000 feet. Although it was under full power, it was hovering dangerously close to a stall as it whirled across the sky in its crazy aerobatic manoeuvre.

Meanwhile, the negative 'g' forces had been playing havoc with the unfortunate navigator, who had been lifted forcefully out of his seat and buffeted painfully against the roof before falling on to the gangway floor. With considerable difficulty, he retrieved his parachute pack – a chest type – and clipped it on to his harness. Then, reconnecting his intercom lead, which had come loose when he parted company with his seat, he asked Ledwidge if it was okay to jettison the door.

'Yes,' the pilot replied, 'but don't go yet.'

The hatch flew away and a quick check satisfied Steward that the windbreak had popped out. Through the open door, he could see a crazy roundabout of sky and earth. There was no time to feel sick.

With the Canberra's altimeter showing 8,000 feet, the speed fell away to only 150 knots as the aircraft wallowed out of another roll. Ledwidge knew that she was going to stall: it was now or never. As the aircraft came the right way up, he yelled: 'Okay – go now!'

Steward disconnected his R/T lead and dived into space. He felt a rush of air, followed by a jolt as his parachute opened. Then he was drifting earthwards, his ears throbbing with the roar of the Canberra's engines as it whirled away.

As soon as he saw that Steward had got out safely, Ledwidge lowered his seat to the position for ejection and pulled the face blind. The seat banged out, separating from the pilot automatically. Both men made a safe landing. Later, Ledwidge's courage in remaining with the crippled aircraft to enable his navigator to escape brought him the award of the Air Force Cross.

Another aircraft with rear-crew escape problems was the Avro Vulcan, the big delta-winged bomber which entered RAF squadron service in 1957 and which, for the next twelve years, formed the backbone of Britain's nuclear deterrent force until that role was taken over by Polaris submarines from 1968. In a Vulcan, the pilot and co-pilot had ejection seats; the other three crew members, two navigators and an air electronics officer, sat facing rearwards at their consoles and had to bale out manually. Although trials with ejection seats for the rear crew were carried out in other aircraft and considerable thought was given to the installation of adequate escape systems, no ejection seats were installed in the Vulcan or the other RAF V-Bombers, the Valiant and Victor, and a number of valuable aircrew were lost as a result.

The deficiency, in fact, was highlighted in dramatic fashion at the very start of the Vulcan's career. On 9 September 1956 one of the first two Vulcan B.1s scheduled for delivery to the RAF took off from Boscombe Down on the first leg of a goodwill flight to New Zealand via Aden, Singapore and Melbourne. The following month, while approaching to land in low cloud and rain at London Airport at the very end of what had been a triumphant tour, it struck the ground short of the runway and rose into the air again, but was so damaged as to be uncontrollable and crashed. The pilot, Squadron Leader Howard, and the co-pilot, Air Marshal Sir Harry Broadhurst – at that time Air Officer Commanding RAF Bomber Command – escaped by using their ejection seats after making futile efforts to regain control; but the two navigators, the air electronics officer and an Avro representative in the rear of the crew compartment lost their lives.

It might easily have been a similar story of tragedy fifteen years later, when Flight Lieutenant Garth Alcock and his four-man crew faced an appalling emergency in a Vulcan B.2 of No. 44 Squadron on 8 January 1971. It happened during a low-level training sortie over Northumberland, when the Vulcan – based at RAF Waddington, in Lincolnshire – began to run into bad weather. Alcock decided to climb out of it, but as the engine power was increased there was a loud explosion and number one engine caught fire, quickly followed by number two engine. The crew took prompt action and reported that the fires appeared to have gone out, so Alcock held the Vulcan in its climb under the power of the two remaining engines and put out a distress call, turning south to head for RAF Leeming in North Yorkshire, a master diversion airfield where there were full crash and rescue facilities.

The labouring bomber reached 6,000 feet, approaching the River Tyne. Things were looking more optimistic; if Alcock could maintain this altitude he should be able to reach Leeming, some sixty miles to the south, in just a few minutes.

Suddenly, the Vulcan's Air Electronics Operator, Flight Lieutenant Jim Power, raised the alarm. The flames had broken out again and part of the underside of the port wing was burning fiercely. Alcock, his hopes of making a safe landing dwindling with every second as the fire spread, flew on until the bomber was clear of cloud and over open country, when he ordered the three rear crew members – Jim Power and the two navigators, Flight Lieutenant James Vinales and Flying Officer Roger Barker – to bale out.

Now only Alcock and his co-pilot, Flying Officer Pete Hoskins, were left. Both had ejection seats, and knew that they could leave the crippled aircraft comparatively fast if they had to. Neither knew how long the Vulcan would stay in the air, or whether it might explode at any moment; the port wing and rear fuselage were now well alight and the bomber was dragging a great banner of smoke in its wake. Yet, although the Vulcan was becoming increasingly difficult to control, Alcock knew that he had to hold on for as long as possible. The bomber was flying near the sprawling, densely populated Tyne area, close to the city of Newcastle and its neighbouring towns of Gateshead and Sunderland, and what might happen if it crashed there did not bear contemplation.

So Alcock and Hoskins remained in the shuddering cockpit for twelve more minutes, fighting together to hold the Vulcan on course, taking it safely over the populated areas and on past the historic city of Durham, turning out at last towards the coast. Pieces of molten, burning wreckage fell from the bomber as it staggered in, and at last Alcock felt his control slipping away. Reluctantly, for there were still some miles to run before he reached the sea, he ordered Hoskins to eject and prepared to follow suit. The Vulcan's cockpit roof flew away with a thud and Hoskins blasted out in his seat, leaving Alcock alone in what was now little more than eighty tons of blazing debris, dazed by the thunder of the airflow and the roar of fuel tanks that were now exploding one after the other.

And still he held on, for a few more desperate seconds, fighting to make sure that the aircraft would come down on open ground before he, too, pulled his seat handle and hurtled from the cockpit. Beneath him, as his parachute deployed, the flaming mass began its last plunge, roaring like a gigantic fireball over the village of Wingate to scatter its wreckage over several fields.

Those last few seconds had been vital. If Alcock had relinquished control just a fraction earlier, the bomber would have plunged into shops and houses. Alcock was subsequently awarded the Air Force Cross, and the other four crew members received the Queen's Commendation for Valuable Service in the Air.

Sometimes a successful ejection has been only the preliminary to a far greater ordeal. Such was the case with Lieutenant David Steeves, a USAF pilot who, on the morning of 9 May 1957, took off in his T-33 jet from Hamilton Air Force Base, California, on a routine training mission. He took the T-33 up to 38,000 feet and levelled off, cruising over the bleak, snow-patched wilderness of the High Sierra mountains. The minutes ticked by; everything was normal.

Then, without warning, Steeves' world exploded. He was slammed brutally forward in his straps and knocked into momentary oblivion. When he came to, the cockpit was full of smoke and the T-33 was spinning wildly. For a few precious seconds he fought to regain control, then, realizing that it was useless, he ejected.

The seat worked perfectly and Steeves was soon swinging under his parachute, conscious only of relief and cold and silence. Then his relief turned to sudden alarm as he felt instinctively that he was falling too fast. Looking up, he saw that two of the canopy's silken panels were torn. There was no time to worry about it now, and certainly nothing he could do about it. The snow-covered mountains seemed to be racing up to meet him. Seconds later, his feet smashed into a rocky ledge and he collapsed in a snow-drift.

Painfully, he dragged himself into a sitting position and explored his injuries. The impact had sprained both his ankles; they had already begun to swell. Apart from that, he appeared to have sustained only a few bruises.

Nevertheless, his position was serious enough. He was in the middle of a barren, icy waste, with nothing in his pockets but a revolver, a couple of half-used books of matches, some money, a pipe but no tobacco, and a photograph of his attractive wife, Rita, and their thirteen-month-old daughter Leisa. To make matters worse, he was wearing only a light summer uniform and was already blue with cold, shivering in the knife-edged wind that came howling down from the north-east.

With the wind came the first flakes of what promised to be a heavy snowfall. Laboriously, Steeves dragged himself into the shelter of some rocks and wrapped himself in the silk of his parachute. He was to remain huddled there for three days, completely without food, quenching his thirst with snow and ice.

By the fourth morning, he knew that there was no hope of rescue. There was only one thing for it : he had to start moving, or die. Gritting his teeth against the pain, he dragged himself to his feet and slowly, his head bowed against the biting wind, he began to stumble through the snow. When night fell, he scooped a hollow in the snow and lay down in it, sodden and weary, wrapped in some fragments of parachute silk he was using as a makeshift cloak. The whole exhausting pattern was repeated the next day . . . and the next . . . and the day after that.

Meanwhile, at her home in Trumbull, Connecticut, Steeves' wife was fighting a heartbreaking struggle against grief and anxiety. She had already received an official telegram, informing her that her husband was missing – and a few days later, a death certificate was issued. But Rita Steeves went on hoping, and waiting.

Towards the evening of his fifteenth day in the wilderness,

Steeves found himself in a canyon – and there, nestling between the sheer walls, was a log cabin. Inside, he found some cans on a shelf, containing ham and beans. There was a packet of dried soup, too, and some sugar. Tears streamed down the pilot's dirty, bearded cheeks as he broke open the cans with the aid of a rusty knife and ate his fill. Then, rolling himself in some sacking, he dropped into a deep, exhausted sleep.

The sun was high when he awoke the following day. Checking his small store of food, he discovered that in his ravenous hunger of the previous night he had eaten more than he had intended. The rest would soon be gone. During the next couple of days, however, Steeves occasionally caught a brief glimpse of deer in the canyon; they seemed to be using a well-trodden path, so the pilot devised a crude trap, lashing his cocked revolver to a sapling with one of his bootlaces and stretching a wire from the trigger to a nearby salt lick. He lined up the revolver carefully, banking on the chance that when one of the animals bent to lick the salt, it would touch the wire and spring the trap, sending a bullet through its head.

The trap worked early one morning, but Steeves failed to hear the shot because he was asleep. By the time he reached the carcass, most of it had been devoured by mountain lions. Nevertheless, he was able to salvage some of the meat, which he cut into strips and ate raw.

On his thirtieth day in the wilderness, Steeves decided that he was strong enough to make another attempt to reach civilization, having obtained some extra rations in the way of trout, wild strawberries and an occasional snake. For two days, he toiled across the side of a mountain, searching for an easy way down, only to find his way barred by a raging torrent, fed by melting snow. He tried to get across, and almost drowned in the act. Utterly dispirited, he had no alternative but to return to his cabin. The daily struggle for food was resumed, and added to this problem was another: the growing fear that he might lose his sanity.

On Sunday, 30th June 1957 – fifty-two days after he had parachuted from his crippled jet – Steeves left the canyon once more, this time heading in a different direction. On the evening of 1 July, after covering about twenty miles, he stumbled on two hunters, enjoying an evening meal by their campfire. The sight of Steeves staggering out of the dusk, his cheeks sunken and raked by thorns, his clothing in tatters, gave them a considerable shock; but they gave him some steak to eat and listened with growing incredulity as he choked out his story between mouthfuls. The next morning they took him to the nearest Air Force base, and to a world which had believed him dead for weeks.

Steeves had been exceptionally lucky to survive – but hardly as fortunate as Lieutenant Tracy B. Mathewson, another USAF pilot who, in the late afternoon of 11 December 1950, was flying in a formation of four F-80 Shooting Star jets on an offensive mission over North Korea.

Racing low over the snowy landscape, the pilots spotted a pair of North Korean Yak-9 fighters climbing away from Pyongyang airport. They seemed an easy target and Mathewson pushed open the throttle, at the same time flicking off the safety-catch of his machine-guns. Perhaps, he thought, this was the moment he had been waiting for: the chance to score his first 'kill' over Korea.

But Mathewson's world suddenly turned upside down as a shattering explosion tore his plane apart. The jet skidded violently across the sky and the pilot was hurled brutally against the side of the cockpit as the fighter flicked over on its back. He snatched a glance rearwards. Where the tail should have been there was nothing; the F-80 had been torn in two.

He had to eject, and fast. He groped for the hood jettison release and pulled it. The perspex canopy flew off with a bang and a blast of air roared into the cockpit, blinding him. The aircraft rolled as another explosion shook it. A dark shadow flashed past the cockpit. It was the wing, torn completely from the fuselage. Frantically, Mathewson groped for the ejection seat handle.

The next instant, without knowing how it had happened, he found himself spreadeagled in mid-air, detached from his seat, falling amid a cloud of débris. Desperately, he tore at his parachute's D-ring. A strip of silk the size of a pocket handkerchief fluttered mockingly from the parachute pack. He had no time to feel fear; there was a hazy impression of the earth whirling up to meet him, a violent shock – and then oblivion.

A few hundred feet above, the other three American jets, the enemy fighters forgotten, swept over the spot where Mathewson had hit the ground and circled the wreck of his F-80. The pilots could see Mathewson's body, his Mae West lifejacket a bright patch of yellow against the churned-up snow and mud. Then, incredibly, they saw the downed pilot sit up and wave to them.

Mathewson released his unopened parachute, scrambled to his feet and felt his body cautiously to see if anything was broken. Miraculously, apart from a dull ache in his back, he did not seem to have been injured. The snow had broken his fall. He saw the crumpled fuselage of his aircraft lying about a hundred yards away and began to walk towards it. As he did so, he was puzzled by a series of sharp cracks. He still had some thirty yards to go when it dawned on him; those cracks were the whiplash reports of rifles.

Mathewson threw himself down under cover, taking out his revolver and preparing to shoot it out with the North Korean soldiers who came running towards him, but his three friends overhead had been keeping a watchful eye on him and now they came screaming down to rake the enemy with accurate machine-gun fire. For ninety minutes, while Mathewson kept his head down, relays of American and Australian fighters flew patrols above him, diving down to shoot up anyone who made a move in his direction. Eventually, a little Stinson rescue plane arrived and landed close by, its pilot braving intense small-arms fire to take Mathewson on board.

Mathewson was soon flying again, but after his seventh combat mission over North Korea severe pains in his neck forced him to visit the flight surgeon. The doctor took one astonished look at the X-ray plates and gave orders that would keep Mathewson in a hospital bed for fourteen months.

He had been flying with a broken neck.

5 The Man Who Flew a Bomb

At 15,000 feet, the cockpit of the big Boeing KC-97G was pleasantly warm. Apart from the readings shown on an outside air temperature gauge, there was no hint that the crew were separated only by the thickness of the aircraft's skin from blistering, sub-zero cold. Far below, the long shadows of the Arctic night hid the vast wastes of Greenland.

In the distance, beyond the curve of the earth, the ghostly veils of the aurora danced and flickered, but the crew took no notice of them. They were all part of the scene in these latitudes; just one factor in an unreal, alien weather pattern where the ionosphere could suddenly go crazy, radio transmissions be blacked out for minutes on end and compass needles spin wildly. It was 27 November 1956, and for the crew of the KC-97G this was just another routine training mission. The big Boeing, callsign 'Turmoil Five', was one of six similar aircraft spaced at intervals through the Arctic darkness, orbiting over fixed positions. All of them belonged to the 26th Air Refuelling Squadron of the USAF, operating out of Thule in Greenland.

In those dangerous years of the mid-1950s, with East-West tension at its height, a new term had come into being: the nuclear deterrent. Twenty-four hours a day, seven days a week, a proportion of Strategic Air Command's mighty bomber fleet patrolled these icy skies, armed with thermonuclear weapons and instantly ready to strike at targets deep in the heart of the Soviet Union should the latter launch a surprise attack. The bombers' life blood during those long hours on patrol was JP-4 fuel, thousands of gallons of it, gulped down by their thirsty turbojets – and supplying that fuel was the task of the flying tankers of the 26th Air Refuelling Squadron, and others like it.

Tonight, the tankers were to make rendezvous with Boeing B-52 Stratofortresses, the giant eight-engined jet bombers which were the latest additions to Strategic Air Command's fleet. It was a task that called for very precise flying on the part of both bomber and tanker pilots; positioning the two aircraft for the transfer of fuel was a tricky process, for there was a considerable speed margin between the B-52 and the much slower, piston-engined KC-97G.

Nevertheless, every member of the tanker crew knew his job backwards, and they all had implicit faith in the skill of their aircraft captain, even though he was a relative newcomer to the flight refuelling business. He was Flight Lieutenant Max Barton of the RAF, an Englishman on a two-year exchange tour with the USAF. Barton had joined the RAF in 1944 at the age of eighteen and had originally trained as a navigator, flying in Lancaster bombers. Demobilised at the end of the war, he had taken a course in aeronautical engineering, after which he had gone to work in the research and development department of A. V. Roe and Company, the British aircraft manufacturers who at that time were designing the radical new delta-winged jet bomber which was to enter service with the RAF in 1957 as the Avro Vulcan. Flying was in his blood, however, and in 1950 the RAF had accepted him back for pilot training. He had graduated from the flying training school at RAF Feltwell with honours, receiving all three of the major trophies awarded to the best student at the end of each course.

All the other members of the KC-97G's crew were Americans. Beside Barton, in the right-hand seat, sat Second Lieutenant 'Nick' Nichols, the co-pilot, and behind them, at their stations on the roomy flight deck, were the navigator, radio operator and flight engineer. Separated from the rest of the crew, surrounded by fuel gauges and pipes in a position near the tail of the aircraft, was the refuelling boom operator.

Barton brought the KC-97G out of its orbit, flying straight

and level at 15,000 feet on a predetermined heading. The navigator, Captain Jim Sullivan, was watching the 'blip' of the approaching B-52 on his radar screen, and passed a steady flow of information about its progress to Barton, who was in radio contact with the bomber. Now, as the B-52 came up astern and below, closing steadily, the boom operator, Staff Sergeant Painter, crept down into a special blister beneath the tanker's rear fuselage. Lying on his stomach in this position, he extended the tanker's long refuelling boom and took over the radio link with the B-52 pilot, guiding the latter into position and manoeuvring the boom until it locked into place in a hatch on top of the bomber's fuselage, behind the cockpit.

Locked together, the two aircraft sped through the freezing night. From the KC-97G's great reservoirs, fuel passed through the boom into the B-52's tanks at the rate of 600 gallons a minute. The radio operator, Staff Sergeant Morris Carmon, had earlier left his place on the flight deck and now stood in the rear fuselage compartment just forward of Painter's position; with the aid of a torch he kept a watchful eye on the spot where the tanker's intricate 'plumbing' merged with the main four-inch fuel pipe. It was Carmon's job, at this stage in the mission, to detect and rectify any minor leaks that might develop as the JP-4 fuel passed through the pipe under high pressure.

It was cold and gloomy in this remote section of the aircraft, with nothing but the throb of the KC-97G's four powerful Pratt and Whitney radial engines for company, but the refuelling exercise was already more than half over and Carmon would soon be back in the warmth of his radio position. Then, as these thoughts were running through his mind, he suddenly heard a noise that made his blood freeze. Loud above the beat of the engines came a powerful hissing sound, like a punctured tyre. An instant later, Carmon gagged as strong JP-4 fumes penetrated his face mask.

Painter smelt it too, and knew what had happened even before Carmon sounded the alarm. Both men turned their oxygen fully on and Painter alerted the pilot, at the same time shutting off the flow of fuel and retracting the boom. He waved it slowly

55

from side to side in front of the B-52 pilot, signalling that contact was to remain broken, and the big bomber moved quickly away.

Up on the flight-deck, Barton rapidly assessed the situation and set emergency procedures in motion. With highly explosive fuel leaking rapidly into the fuselage, the slightest spark could turn the big aircraft into a ball of fire, so the first task was to switch off the main electricity supply. Barton quickly selected a power setting of nineteen inches manifold pressure and set the engine revolutions to 1,900 rpm. Then he ordered the flight engineer to throw the master-switch.

Instantly, every control and instrument that depended on the KC-97G's main electrical supply ceased to function. Radio and intercom went dead, and the needles of most of the instruments on Barton's panel dropped to zero. Reduced panel lighting and three instruments – the artificial horizon, turn and slip indicator and directional gyro – were kept going by the emergency power supply. The heating also failed and Barton no longer had any control over the pitch of the aircraft's propellers. This, together with the fact that the flaps were also inoperative, would make a landing extremely tricky. Navigation back to base would also be a problem, for Jim Sullivan's radar and radio aids were useless.

Barton had taken the precaution of de-pressurising the cabin, and now he ordered the crew to jettison the hatches in the hope that the noxious fumes might blow away. A howling, icy gale blasted into the fuselage as the hatches whirled away.

Jim Sullivan, using dead reckoning, quickly worked out a rough course for Thule, which was some 250 miles away, and passed his calculations to Barton. The latter turned the tanker on to the new heading and descended cautiously to 10,000 feet. Meanwhile, in the rear of the aircraft, Painter and Carmon were already up to their ankles in JP-4 as they searched for the leak. The hiss of escaping fuel was deafening, and despite their oxygen supply the men were sickened by the smell.

It was Painter who found the leak – an X-shaped rupture about three inches across in one of the pipes. Through it, fuel was spurting into the fuselage at fifty gallons a minute. Instantly, Painter knew that there was no possibility of repairing the damage. Followed by Carmon, he went forward to report to the aircraft captain. With the intercom useless, conversation was difficult; the men had to remove their oxygen masks and shout a few words at one another, then replace their masks quickly before the fumes overwhelmed them.

Barton made a quick reappraisal of the situation. There were already hundreds of gallons of fuel sloshing about in the fuselage, pouring from the KC-97G's upper tanks, and the aircraft's main electrical connection box was practically submerged. Any spark would certainly cause a devastating explosion. Barton was literally flying a bomb. To make matters worse, the weight of loose fuel was beginning to affect the trim of the aircraft; anything other than the gentlest of control movements would cause the JP-4 to rush either fore or aft and make the KC-97G critically unstable. There was another worry, too; the loss of electrical power meant that the de-icing equipment no longer worked, and the risk of airframe and engine icing grew with every minute the tanker remained in the air.

Barton knew that some attempt had to be made to drain the growing volume of fuel from the aircraft, so he ordered three of the crew members to go aft and jettison the rear exit door in the hope that the JP-4 would flow out. They waded through the freezing, stinking liquid only to find that fuel had seeped round the edges of the door and frozen solid. Not daring to use axes in case they caused a lethal spark, they spent several minutes trying vainly to dislodge the door. It was hopeless. They came forward again, exhausted with the cold and their exertions, their senses reeling with the fumes.

Jim Sullivan, working hard at his plotting table with the aid of a flashlight, was continually passing course corrections to the pilot. Barton, although finding that controlling the aircraft needed all his concentration, was now fairly certain that he could reach Thule. One by one, he called the other members of the crew up to the cockpit and gave them a choice; either they could stay with the aircraft as he rode it down for a dangerous landing, or they could take to their parachutes when he flew over the airfield. Baling out into the darkness over frozen, rocky ground would be risky, but by now the men were glad of any chance to get away from the awful fumes. They all decided to jump except Nichols, who elected to stay with Barton.

'Thanks a lot, Nick,' the pilot said simply. 'I'd appreciate that.'

The KC-97G droned on through the night, the men on the flight-deck straining their eyes for the glimmer of light that was their base. After an hour, a shout of relief went up as they caught sight of a faint glow, a long way off and to the right, reflected from a thin layer of cloud. It had to be Thule; there were no other lights for hundreds of miles.

Barton's problems, however, were only just beginning. The next task was to lower the aircraft's undercarriage, and without electrics it had to be wound down manually. The whole thing had to be done by operating a series of cranks and levers all in strict order – and, in the darkness, it was several minutes before the job was finished. Even now, the pilot had no way of knowing whether the undercarriage was locked in position, for the loss of the electrics meant that the three green lights that normally showed on his instrument panel were absent.

Barton ordered the crew to put on their parachute packs and began a slow, cautious descent to 5,000 feet, turning gently towards the airfield. He reduced the airspeed to 160 mph; without flaps, he dared go no slower. Very precisely, he lined up with Thule's main runway and then indicated to the men in the fuselage that it was time to jump. One by one, with difficulty because of the slipstream, they made their exits into the darkness.

Now only Barton and Nichols were left, and it seemed very lonely in the large, vibrating cockpit. Barton brought the tanker round in a wide turn, circling the airfield to approach the runway for a landing. He had to get everything right first time, for any sudden increase of power or abrupt change of trim would cause the tons of fuel to shift and result in disaster.

Suddenly, the panel lighting went out. The emergency electrical supply was exhausted, and now he was left only with the airspeed indicator and turn and slip indicator. Barton thanked God that Nichols had stayed behind, for he was able to read the last two working instruments only with the aid of a pocket torch which the co-pilot focused on them.

The KC-97G thundered down through the night towards Thule's main runway. Although the temperature in the cockpit was far below freezing, sweat poured down the faces of both men. Barton had never attempted a landing in a heavily-laden aircraft with no flaps, and his mind was working overtime. He had no idea of the tanker's all-up weight, a crucial factor when working out the best approach speed. At best, he could only compromise. He decided to maintain 160 mph all the way down the approach, reducing to 145 mph as they crossed the runway threshold. In layman's terms, that meant that the big aircraft would be touching down as fast as a jet fighter. Although the runway was 10,000 feet long, he realized that he might not be able to stop the tanker before it careered off the far end. He also knew that if he held the nose too high on the final approach, the tons of fuel in the rear would swirl backwards and send the aircraft out of control – but he would have to raise the nose to kill some of the speed.

As 'Turmoil Five' continued her long, flat approach towards the runway threshold, rescue services on the airfield – alerted by the parachuting crew members – were going into action. Sirens wailed as ambulances and fire tenders raced round the perimeter track and took station beside the runway.

In the aircraft's cockpit, Barton had eyes only for the lights ahead as Nichols called out the airspeed by the light of his torch. Vaguely, the pilot was aware of the darkened landscape, sweeping past beneath the tanker's wings. He realized that he was a little high, so he shouted to Nichols to reduce the power a fraction. The co-pilot complied instantly, easing back the throttles, and the aircraft sank a couple of hundred feet.

The runway threshold was coming up fast now, and Barton – very, very gently – began to apply backward pressure to the control column. Beside him, Nichols continued to call out the speed. 'One-fifty . . . one forty-five . . . one forty-five . . . one-forty . . . one-forty . . . one thirty-five . . .'

She was floating, her main undercarriage skimming the surface of the runway. Barton raised the nose a fraction higher and a moment later felt a heavy jolt as the wheels finally touched. He knew that behind him, the mass of JP-4 would be flowing towards the rear of the fuselage and that he had to get the nose down, for if the tail scraped against the concrete the resulting friction would blow them to kingdom come. Firmly, he shoved the control column forward.

Nothing happened. The runway raced beneath them at 200 feet per second and still the nose remained obstinately in the air. Barton went on pushing, his arms rigid and the sweat standing out in beads on his brow.

If they were not to finish up as a pile of burning wreckage among the rocks at the far end of the runway, he had to use the brakes. But the speed was still 100 mph, and the KC-97G's handling notes forbade the use of brakes above 60 mph. To apply them now risked having the undercarriage collapse, and if that happened it would be all over. In a fraction of a second, Barton weighed up the alternatives and made his decision. As the tanker careered down the icy runway like a juggernaut, leaving the racing fire-tenders and ambulances far behind, he trod gently, just for a split second, on the mainwheel brake pedals. It was the merest touch, but it was enough. The wheels locked a fraction and the nose began to come down, slowly and reluctantly. A second later, the nosewheel's comforting rumble sounded on the runway.

Barton was able to use the brakes fully now, and gradually the big aircraft lost its momentum. It finally came to a stop three-quarters of the way down the runway. For a few moments Barton and Nichols sat unmoving, scarcely able to believe that they had got down safely. Then Nichols let out his pent-up breath with an explosive gasp and the two men relaxed, grinning at each other.

Even now, the danger was not over. As they left their seats, Barton noticed fuel seeping under the forward escape hatch. Not daring to risk any friction, the two men decided to make their exit through an emergency hatch on the flight deck. Someone on the ground tossed them a rope and they slid down it.

To his immense relief, Barton learned that all his crew had

landed safely. Then, as he turned to inspect the aircraft, he realized how lucky he and Nichols had been. Fuel was pouring out of every crevice and wisps of smoke still curled from the mainwheels, the result of the heavy braking during the last few hundred yards of the landing run. Fortunately, no fuel had come into contact with the hot undercarriage units.

On 13 July 1957 Major General Sweeney, Commander of the United States Eighth Air Force, presented Flight Lieutenant Max Barton with a rare award for an RAF officer; the American Distinguished Flying Cross for outstanding bravery in the air.

6 Escape from the East

The young airman drifted up from the depths of sleep and turned over to look at the clock on his bedside table. It was 6 am. Stretching, he threw aside the blankets and jumped out of bed, then walked quickly over to the window. It was a beautiful September morning, the air crystal-clear and fresh with the tang of early autumn. Perfect flying weather, he thought, as he ran some hot water for his morning shave.

A lieutenant in the Polish Air Force, Zygmunt Gosciniak was known to his superiors as a good communist. It was an attitude he had cultivated ever since he had entered the basic flying school at Deblin in 1952. For a young officer in Soviet-dominated Poland, membership of the communist party was the only road to success, and flying ability came second to political 'awareness'. But being a communist in Poland had its advantages; one had a greater margin of freedom, for example, and a man in Gosciniak's position – he was secretary of the local communist party branch, as well as deputy chairman of the political section at Zegrze Pomorski airfield, where he was based – had the trust of his superiors.

Gosciniak swore as the razor slipped, nicking his chin slightly. The hand that held the razor was trembling, and there was a tight knot in his stomach. He paused and stared at his reflection in the mirror, willing his nerves to calm down. Then he finished his shave, dressed, and took a sheaf of papers from the drawer of a bureau. For a few minutes he sifted through them, extracting some and putting them in the pockets of his tunic.

At 7.30, a car horn sounded twice in the street outside.

63

Gosciniak paused at the door and looked back at the room. It was small – just a bed-sitter in a large house occupied mainly by Polish military personnel – but it had been his home for the past couple of years, and he knew that whatever happened during the next few hours he would never see it again.

For today, 25 September 1956, Lieutenant Zygmunt Gosciniak – a politically sound and invaluable member of the Polish Communist Party, according to his file – was going to try to escape from Poland.

For four years he had been planning this escape. Four years during which he had built up a façade of trustworthiness, gradually earning the respect of his superiors. Four years of waiting for the best opportunity. His plans were really quite simple. A hundred miles away, a mere twelve or thirteen minutes' flying time away from Zegrze Pomorski, lay the Danish island of Bornholm. When his compatriots were least expecting it, Gosciniak planned to fly his aircraft across those few miles of sea to freedom. On the surface, it seemed simple enough; all he had to do was break away during a training flight, push the nose of his jet fighter down to gain maximum speed, and head for the coast at low level. But two Russian fighters always patrolled the coastline as a safeguard against just such an attempt, and the coast was heavily defended by anti-aircraft batteries. He would need a lot of luck to get through in one piece. Apart from that, the Polish pilots were allowed just enough fuel to carry out their training missions, so there would be no margin for error.

Also, there were his friends to be considered. Up to now, Gosciniak had always flown with other Polish pilots. He could have made his dash for freedom on several occasions, but had he done so his friends might have been accused of co-operating with him, and they would have been given little chance to prove their innocence.

Today, however, it was different. This morning, Gosciniak was detailed to fly with a Russian Air Force officer who was attached to the Polish squadron as an ' adviser '. In fact, it was the Russian who really ran the unit, and the Polish commanding officer never dared to question his decisions.

The car took Gosciniak to the officers' mess and he went into the dining-room to have breakfast. The Russian was already there and Gosciniak sat down opposite him; the previous evening, the two had arranged to meet over breakfast to discuss tactics. Gosciniak knew that he must show no sign of nervousness, so he ordered a large meal and forced himself to eat heartily, even though his stomach was turning over. Half-way through, he suddenly pushed his plate aside and took a long drink of coffee; if he had eaten another forkful, he would have been violently sick all over the table. The Russian glanced at him curiously and asked him if he was feeling unwell. Gosciniak made some excuse to account for his lack of appetite; his table companion shrugged, apparently satisfied, and returned to their discussion.

At ten o'clock, the two men collected their flying kit and walked out to where their MiG-15 jet fighters stood ready on the flight line. Gosciniak's ground-crew chief grinned at him as he came up.

'Everything's okay, sir,' he said. 'You're lucky to have this aircraft.'

You'll never know how lucky, Gosciniak thought as he surveyed his fighter. It was one of the brand new MiG-15B jets which had been recently delivered to the squadron, and its performance was better than the aircraft the Russian was flying. It would also give him a better chance of survival if he had to run the gauntlet of any patrols.

Gosciniak completed his external inspection of the fighter and began to climb into the cockpit. Suddenly he hesitated. On an impulse, he took off his wristwatch and handed it to the crew chief. 'Here,' he said. 'I want you to keep this as a memento in case I get killed.'

The crew chief looked at him in surprise, but said nothing. He took the watch and held it for a long moment before slipping it into his pocket.

Damn, thought Gosciniak, whatever made me do that? He was almost certain that the man knew that something was wrong. But he made no sign that he had guessed the truth.

There was no time for self-recrimination now. Gosciniak

settled down in the cockpit and began his starting-up checks. The turbojet came to life with its characteristic strident whine and the two MiGs idled round the perimeter track, lining up on the runway with the Russian some distance ahead of Gosciniak's aircraft. Then the two pilots opened the throttles and the fighters thundered away, curving out from the airfield on a north-easterly heading and entering a steady climb to 20,000 feet.

The air exercise involved simulated attack and evasion, the pilots recording each other's performance with their camera guns. Ironically, Gosciniak found himself simulating the role of an 'enemy' pilot, trying to escape from the Russian's attack. Then the roles were reversed, with the Pole acting as the attacker.

The Russian's voice crackled in Gosciniak's earphones. 'All right, now it's your turn. Stand by to carry out a practice interception. I will be the target. I am peeling off to port – now!'

Gosciniak was flying a couple of thousand feet lower than the Russian, temporarily out of sight of the Soviet instructor. He watched as the other pilot broke away in a diving turn to the left, and realized that this was his big chance. Rolling the MiG over on its back, he went down in a screaming dive in the opposite direction. The speed crept up past the 600 mph mark and the aircraft began to vibrate. Gently, Gosciniak eased back the stick and brought the fighter out of its dive at 400 feet, hopping over trees, buildings and hedgerows as he headed for the coast.

The pilots had been carrying out their exercise only twenty-five miles from the sea. Now, as the coastline came up to meet him, Gosciniak heard the Russian's frantic call over the radio:

'Number Two, where are you? I have lost contact!'

Gosciniak took a deep breath and pressed the R/T button. 'Number Two calling. I have lost contact and am making for point B.'

To the Russian, point B meant Belgard, a prearranged rendezvous in case the fighters lost touch with each other. For Gosciniak, however, point B had taken on a new significance: Bornholm.

The MiG sped over the coast without opposition, but Gosciniak soon ran into difficulties. After flying for about two minutes over the sea, he discovered that his compass was not working properly, so he had to climb – risking radar detection – to get his bearings. Relief flooded through his body as he located the island, but was quickly replaced by other anxieties. He had no idea whether there was an airstrip there, and did not know how he would be received even if he managed to put down in one piece. His hand caressed the revolver he had hidden in his flying overall before take-off. Even suicide was preferable to the slow death he was bound to suffer if he were sent back to Poland.

As Bornholm came up under the nose, he searched desperately for somewhere to land. Then he saw it : a scar on the drab landscape, easily distinguishable to a pilot as a runway. Lowering the undercarriage and flaps, he made a quick check on the wind direction and began his approach to land, hardly daring to hope that he had achieved his goal at last.

As the MiG came down through 200 feet, Gosciniak suddenly saw a dark blotch on the runway ahead of him. In a split second, he realized that he was looking at a group of workmen. Pushing open the throttle, he pulled back the stick and roared over their heads. As he flashed overhead, he could see their white, upturned faces staring up at him. Obstinately, they refused to budge from their position.

Gosciniak climbed and circled the airstrip, firing some flares. Still the men would not move. A glance at the fuel gauge showed him that he had just enough left to attempt a landing. All right, he thought : since I can't land on the runway, I'll have to try and bring her down for a belly-landing on the grass.

Retracting his undercarriage, he pulled a lever and the cockpit canopy flew off with a bang. That way, it would be easier for him to get out if he wrecked the fighter on touchdown. He throttled back and started his approach, leap-frogging over a house which momentarily obscured his view. Then, to his horror, he saw a new danger : right in his path stood a bulldozer. Frantically, he kicked the rudder bar and the MiG slewed to the left. The port wingtip struck the ground with a jarring crunch, flinging him forward in his straps. His head smashed sickeningly against the gunsight.

The MiG had hit the ground at 150 miles an hour. Dragging a mighty banner of dust, it scraped and skidded across the sun-parched grass, throwing the pilot around like a rag doll in the cockpit.

Then, suddenly, there was silence. Dazed, Gosciniak undid his straps and climbed out on to the wing. Through the dust of his crash-landing he saw a group of men running towards him. They were shouting : he didn't understand the language, but he didn't care. It was the language of freedom.

Ahead of Gosciniak now, after interrogation, lay the beginning of a new life in England. He had been lucky, for he had left behind no dependent relatives and the ties that bound him to his homeland were few.

Other would-be escapers were not so fortunate. One of them was Ladislaw Bezak, a senior captain with Czechoslovak Airlines, who determined to make a bid for freedom with his wife and four children in December 1971. In fact, Bezak had been planning his escape since August 1968, when Soviet tanks rolled into Prague and robbed the Czech people of the brief, heady taste of liberty they had enjoyed under Prime Minister Dubcek.

His plans were finally completed in the autumn of 1971. He knew that there was only a slender chance of getting away, but he was determined that his children would not spend another Christmas in austere, communist-dominated Czechoslovakia. All he needed was the opportunity.

Shortly after noon on Sunday, 19 December, he drove to Kladno airport, twenty miles from Prague. It was here that he kept the little Zlin light aircraft; even though commercial flying was his business, he still enjoyed taking the little plane for an hour's joyride on a Sunday afternoon, and he was well known to the airport staff.

Fighting down his tension, he checked out with air traffic control, telling them that he was going for an hour's local flying. No one suspected anything as the Zlin bumped over the grass and took off. As soon as he was out of sight of the airfield Bezak came down low, skimming over the familiar landscape. After a few minutes he spotted what he was looking for – a small field, bordered by a wood.

Skilfully, he brought the little aircraft in to land, skipping over a high fence and touching down on the uneven surface. As the Zlin rolled to a stop, Bezak's 27-year-old wife Maria, carrying two-year-old Andre and accompanied by Ladislaw, eight, and seven-year-old twins Martin and Roman, emerged from the trees. Hurriedly, the family climbed into the rear cockpit; five people in a tiny, cramped space designed only for one.

Bezak taxied back to the boundary to give himself the longest possible take-off run. Turning into wind, he opened the throttle wide, sending the Zlin lurching across the grass. Fifty yards . . . a hundred. The tail came up and the overladen aircraft bounced a few feet into the air, then came down again. The fence on the far side of the airfield loomed closer. Sweating, Bezak pulled back the stick as the Zlin lurched into the air again, but it refused to gain height. As the wheels touched the ground once more, he closed the throttle and applied the brakes, bringing the aircraft to a stop only feet from the fence.

He taxied back across the field and tried again, with the same result. In despair, he told his wife and children to get out. A new plan was already forming in his mind.

He took off alone and flew back to Kladno. There, he told the controllers that he would be flying again later that afternoon. Then he ran to his car and drove at breakneck speed to pick up his family. He had decided to risk everything on a crazy gamble.

Within an hour he was once again climbing into the cockpit of his Zlin, this time with his family hidden in bushes near the end of the runway. His heart pounding, he taxied out along the perimeter track towards the runway end; this alone should have been enough to make the controllers suspicious, because he normally used the grass for taking off. The Zlin was not fitted with radio, but at any moment Bezak expected to see a red flare rise from the control tower, or an airport security car racing after him.

Nothing happened. Stopping just short of the runway, Bezak turned the Zlin broadside on so that its fuselage hid the bushes where his family crouched. His wife and children ran out and scrambled into the narrow cockpit and Bezak turned quickly on to the runway, opening the throttle and sending the Zlin racing down the tarmac. In the rear cockpit, his family crouched as low as possible to try and avoid being seen.

The Zlin staggered into the air, clawing for altitude under the extra weight. To avoid suspicion, Bezak turned in the direction of the East German border until Kladno was out of sight, then he pointed the aircraft towards Western Germany. The miles slid by; Bezak and Maria began to relax and the children, not understanding what was at stake, chattered excitedly to one another. Pilsen lay over to the left, which meant that only about thirty miles separated them from the frontier.

Suddenly, the Zlin lurched violently and a dark shadow sped over the cockpit. Bezak fought to regain control and looked up. Ahead and above a MiG-17 jet rocketed skywards, buffeting the Zlin in its slipstream. The jet turned and came diving down again, a deadly arrow that grew bigger with terrifying speed.

There was a slim chance the fighter pilot was having fun. Maybe the alarm had not been raised and the MiG had not been sent out to intercept the fugitive, after all. Bezak waggled the Zlin's wings and waved; the next instant, he was fighting for his family's life as a stream of glowing cannon shells flashed across the light aircraft's nose.

Bezak knew instantly that only his skill as a pilot could save them now. Ten years earlier, he had risen to flying fame as a world aerobatic champion. He could do everything with a Zlin, which was probably the finest aerobatic plane in the world, except make it talk. But that had been ten years ago, and he had never been forced to loop, roll and spin with his wife and children in the rear cockpit, and the lives of all of them at stake.

There was no alternative. As the MiG came in for another firing pass, Bezak launched into the craziest aerobatic sequence of his career. Behind him, the children screamed as the earth gyrated round them and they were flung around the cockpit. Maria clung frantically to little Andre and tried to brace herself as best she could. Although none of them was strapped in, they were wedged tightly together. This fact alone prevented them from being knocked unconscious against the perspex – or hurled through it.

The MiG pilot, taken by surprise, overshot and his shells went far wide of their target. As he climbed away for another try, Bezak pushed down the Zlin's nose and headed flat out for a layer of cloud that hung low over the border. The MiG came arrowing down a third time, and once again Bezak was forced to hurl the little aircraft around the sky. Again, the fighter pilot misjudged and again Bezak entered a headlong dive towards the sheltering cloud. Next time, he knew there would be no escape. He had to reach the cloud before the next attack came.

The cries of the children were drowned by the scream of the overworked engine as the Zlin hurtled earthwards at more than 200 miles an hour, vibrating madly. Behind the fleeing aircraft, the MiG was turning in for another attack. There was a brief flurry of cannon fire as the MiG pilot opened up at extreme range – and then the Zlin plunged into the swirling grey sanctuary of the cloud.

The airspeed indicator was off the clock and the needle of the altimeter unwound with terrifying speed. Carefully, conscious that a sudden manoeuvre at this speed and with this load on board might tear off the wings, Bezak eased back the stick. The whole aircraft shuddered and groaned alarmingly as it slowly came out of its dizzy plunge. Suddenly, it burst out of the cloud layer less than 300 feet from the ground.

Bezak glanced back; there was no sign of the fighter. Then he looked down, and almost wept with relief. Unfolding beneath him was the rolling, forest-clad landscape of Bavaria.

Happily, he set course for the airfield at Nuremberg. It was only six days to Christmas. For Bezak and his family, it would be the most memorable Christmas ever, with the most precious gifts imaginable : their lives and their freedom.

7 The High Cold War

On the morning of 2 September 1958 a four-engined Lockheed C-130 Hercules transport of the United States Air Force took off from the NATO air base at Adana, in southern Turkey, and set course north-westwards. The C-130 was attached to the 7406th Support Squadron and was normally based at Rhein-Main Air Base near Frankfurt, Western Germany.

The Lockheed Hercules, which had first entered service with the USAF's Military Air Transport Service in December 1956, was an amazingly versatile aircraft, able to carry a wide variety of cargoes and to operate, if necessary, out of rough airstrips anywhere in the world. It was still to be the workhorse of America's air transport fleet, and the principal transport aircraft of many other air forces too, a quarter of a century later.

On that September day in 1958, however, the C-130 cruising over the mountains of Turkey carried a strange cargo. Its spacious fuselage was packed with advanced electronic equipment and it carried a crew of seventeen men, thirteen of whom were radio and radar specialists. Their mission was to intercept and identify signals from the network of Soviet radar stations to the north of the Black Sea and in Armenia and Georgia; signals that would tell them not only what type of radar was being used, but also reveal its range and other information.

The first leg of the C-130's flight took it high over the 12,000-foot peaks of the Canik mountains. Ninety minutes and 350 miles out from Adana the aircraft was over Trabzon, on the north coast of Turkey, and the pilot, Captain Paul E. Duncan, turned right through ninety degrees and headed for Lake Van, 250 miles away in the south-east corner of Turkey. This new heading took the Hercules parallel with the border of Soviet Armenia, which was about a hundred miles away off the aircraft's port wing.

The Hercules never reached Lake Van, and an extensive search for it all over eastern Turkey revealed nothing. On 6 September, after considerable discussion, the American Embassies in Moscow and Teheran formally asked the Russians and Iranians if the aircraft had come down in their territory, having strayed over the border by accident; both denied all knowledge of its fate.

Then, on 12 September, the Soviet Foreign Ministry stated that the wreckage of an American military aircraft had been discovered in Soviet Armenia, some thirty-five miles north of the town of Yerevan, and that six badly mutilated bodies had been recovered. The Russians claimed that the aircraft had deliberately violated their air space, an allegation which – in view of the circumstances surrounding the C-130's mission – the Americans naturally denied. The next day, in fact, the American chargé d'affaires in Moscow handed a note to the Soviet Foreign Ministry, alleging that the Hercules had been intercepted by Soviet fighters close to the Turkish-Armenian border, that the American pilot had obeyed the fighters' instructions to follow them eastwards, but that his aircraft had been deliberately destroyed shortly afterwards. It was claimed that eye-witnesses on the Turkish side of the border had seen the Hercules turn towards the east; soon afterwards, they had heard an explosion and had observed a column of smoke rising from a point within the Soviet territory. These allegations were flatly denied by the Russians.

Then the Americans played their trump card. Monitoring stations in Turkey, they stated, had made a tape-recording from the Soviet fighter frequency of what appeared to be the R/T chatter between four Russian pilots. The date and time of the transmission tallied exactly with that of the C-130's disappearance, and the translated text of the Russians' conversation, as released by the USAF, was as follows:

'I see the target, to the right!'

'I see the target.'

'Roger.'

'The target is a big one.'

'Attack by four-fourths.'

'Roger.'

'The target is a four-engined transport.'

'Target speed is three-zero-zero. I am going along with it. It is turning towards the fence.'

At this point the transmission became garbled, the voices of the Russian pilots high-pitched and excited. Then :

'The target is burning.'

'There's a hit.'

'The target is burning, 582.'

'281, are you attacking?'

'Yes, yes, I . . .' (transmission garbled).

'The target is burning . . . the tail assembly is falling off the target. 582, can you see me? I am in front of the target.'

'Look! Look at him, he will not get away, he is already falling.'

'Yes, he is falling. I will finish him off, boys, I will finish him off on this run.'

'The target has lost control. It is going down.'

'The target has turned over . . . aha, you see, it is falling!'

'All right, form up, head for home.'

'The target started burning after my third pass . . .'

The Americans, however, still made no admission that the Hercules had actually penetrated Soviet air space, but there was no longer any doubt that this had happened when, on 24 September, the Russians – who had dismissed the tape-recording as a crude fabrication – returned the bodies of the six crew members, only four of which could be identified. No other bodies were handed over, despite repeated American requests. The US Deputy Under-Secretary of State, Robert Murphy, subsequently issued a statement to the effect that 'the American pilot, as a result of signals transmitted by radio beacons in Soviet Georgia and Armenia, had probably made a navigational error which resulted in his unintentionally crossing the Soviet border.' The statement went on to claim that the Hercules had then been fired on by Soviet aircraft and destroyed.

In fact, the statement implied that the C-130 had been deliberately lured over the border by false radio signals and then shot down. If Captain Paul Duncan had been relying on his radio navigation aids rather than on visual navigation – which was likely, since significant landmarks in the rugged terrain of northeast Turkey were few, and in any case the C-130 was over cloud during the last leg of its flight – then the Russians could have jammed the Lake Van radio beacon transmissions and superimposed their own. A few degrees' deviation from its planned course would have been enough to take the Hercules over Soviet territory. It is likely that Paul Duncan realized his mistake only when the Soviet fighters appeared, and that he immediately turned west towards the frontier – but by then it was too late.

Then, in October, came another extraordinary twist to what was already a bizarre story. *Sovietskaya Aviatsiya*, the daily newspaper of the Red Air Force, published an article purporting to describe an 'air exercise' in which four Soviet jet fighters shot down an 'intruding enemy aircraft'. Significantly, the call-signs of two of the fighters mentioned in the article were identical with those on the American tape; courses and altitudes were also similar. According to the article, the four fighters were 'scrambled' from separate airfields with an interval of several minutes between each pair and were guided to the target by two fighter controllers, Major Kulikov and Captain Romanyuta. The call-signs of the leading pair of fighters (which were unidentified, but probably MiG-17s) were 582 and 281. They were flown by Lieutenants Lopatkov and Gavrilov. The article stated that by the time the second pair of fighters arrived on the scene, their take-off having been delayed by a sandstorm, Lopatkov and Gavrilov had already made three passes at the target and set it on fire. The work of destruction was completed by the other two pilots, Lieutenants Kucheryayev and Ivanov.

Whether the events described in the *Sovietskaya Aviatsiya* article bore any relation to the destruction of the ill-fated Hercules could, of course, never be proved. Two facts, however, were unshakeable. The first was that the Hercules had crashed in Soviet territory, and the second was that it had been engaged in an Elint (Electronic Intelligence) operation.

The gathering of electronic intelligence dates back to the earliest days of radar, and became a key factor in the air operations of both sides during World War II. In 1942, for example, knowledge of the frequencies on which German search and tracking radars operated enabled the British to develop effective countermeasures against them. Not only was such knowledge vital to the effectiveness of the Allied strategic bombing offensive, but it also contributed in no small measure to the success of the Allied landings in Normandy. On 5 June 1944, two squadrons of RAF Lancasters flew fixed patterns over the English Channel for several hours, dropping bundles of ' window ' – strips of tinfoil cut exactly to the wavelength of the German radar – and succeeded in making the enemy believe that the D-Day invasion was taking place miles from the actual landing zones.

With the advent of more advanced radar systems after 1945 the gathering of electronic intelligence assumed even greater importance, and the probing of the other side's radar defences by the Russians and the Western Allies subsequently became a vital aspect of the cold war. It was not without its cost; between 1945 and 1960, the Americans lost at least fifteen aircraft and sixty-nine aircrew on operations of this type. Here are some of the recorded incidents :

On 8 April 1950 a PB4Y Privateer of US Navy Patrol Squadron VP-26, with ten men on board, was shot down by Soviet fighters over the Baltic. There were no survivors.

On 18 January 1953 a Lockheed P2V Neptune of Navy Squadron VP-22, on an Elint mission over the Formosa Strait, was shot down off Swatow Island by Red Chinese anti-aircraft fire. Rescue operations were hampered by shore battery gunfire and high seas, the latter causing a Coast Guard rescue aircraft to crash on take-off. Total losses from the incident were eleven men, seven of them from the P2V crew.

On 29 July 1953 a USAF RB-50 operating out of Yokota Air Base in Japan was attacked by Soviet MiG-15s at 0615 hours while cruising at 21,000 feet over the Sea of Japan, forty miles from the Russian coast over international waters. The RB-50's gunners returned the fire, but one wing of the American aircraft broke away and it spun towards the sea, breaking up as it fell. One crew member escaped by parachute and was picked up by an American destroyer after drifting for several hours in his life-raft; the other fourteen perished.

On 9 September 1954 a P2V Neptune of the US Navy's Patrol Squadron 19, on an intelligence-gathering mission over international waters, was attacked by two MiG-15s and forced to ditch off the Siberian coast. Nine of the crew escaped and were subsequently rescued, but one was lost with the aircraft. On 22 June the following year, another P2V Neptune, this time belonging to the US Navy's VP-9 Squadron, was attacked by two MiG-15s while patrolling the Aleutians area; the fighters set fire to the Neptune's starboard engine and forced the aircraft to crash-land on St Lawrence Island. Fortunately, there were no casualties.

On 22 August 1956 a long-range Martin P4M Mercator, with thirteen men on board, while on night patrol out of Iwakuni, Japan, reported that it was under attack by aircraft over international waters, thirty-two miles off the coast of China, and was not heard from again. Aircraft and surface ships, carrying out an intensive search, found wreckage, empty life rafts and the bodies of two crew members. The Mercator belonged to Electronic Countermeasures Squadron VQ-1, which had been formed a year earlier.

The high proportion of US Navy aircraft involved in these incidents was explained by the fact that the USN's Elint missions were usually flown over the sea, whereas USAF missions were flown over the territory of NATO or other Allied countries around the periphery of the Soviet Union. Aircraft over the sea were vulnerable to interception and attack, and there were seldom survivors or witnesses. Interceptions over land produced all manner of complications, as the Hercules incident of 2 September 1958 showed.

At this time the Russians were extremely touchy about American intelligence-gathering operations, and the reason was not hard to find. In the spring of 1956, a USAF unit known as the 1st Weather Observation Squadron (Provisional) at Watertown, Nevada, had received the first examples of a radical new aircraft that was to alter the whole concept of air reconnaissance : the Lockheed U-2. Virtually a powered glider, with a wingspan of eighty feet and fitted with a modified version of the well-tried J-57 jet engine, the U-2 was the answer to an urgent USAF requirement for an aircraft capable of making deep penetrations into Soviet territory at an altitude that would make it immune from interception by the fighters then in service.

The initial production batch of ten U-2s was in fact used for high-altitude weather reconnaissance and sampling of radiation in the upper atmosphere, but subsequent aircraft were assigned to the 4028th and 4080th Strategic Reconnaissance Squadrons of Strategic Air Command. These squadrons were based on Laughlin Air Force Base in Texas and Ramey AFB in Puerto Rico, but detachments were sent to Lakenheath in Britain, Wiesbaden in Germany and Incirlik in Turkey, and during the autumn of 1956 a series of probing flights was carried out over the fringes of Soviet territory from these bases. When these preliminary flights ended without incident, the U-2s began to undertake deep penetration flights into the heart of the Soviet Union, photographing air bases, missile sites under construction, factories, industrial complexes, radar sites and other objectives of interest to Strategic Air Command's target planners.

Throughout 1957 the U-2s cruised singly over the Soviet Union at altitudes of up to 80,000 feet, apparently undetected by the Soviet defences. Because of the extreme heights at which they flew, their turbojets were fed by a specially-developed fuel, with a boiling point of 150° C at sea level. Early U-2As had a range of about 2,000 miles, but later-model U-2Bs could fly 4,000 miles with the help of underwing fuel tanks. Under operational conditions, range could also be extended by deliberately flaming-out the J-75 turbojet and gliding for long distances, the engine being restarted only when the aircraft reached a dangerously low level. On one occasion, a U-2 on an air test over the

Caribbean Sea from its base on Puerto Rico suffered an engine failure and made a successful emergency landing on Bermuda after gliding 300 miles.

By 1958 the Russians were clearly aware of the U-2s' flights, for fighters were sent up to intercept the elusive American aircraft. U-2 pilots began to report attempted interceptions by MiG-19s and the latest MiG-21s, but the Soviet fighters were unable to reach the heights at which the U-2s operated. They would zoom-climb to 70,000 feet, fire their cannon at the top of the trajectory, then stall in the thin air and fall away. Yet, because of the severe loss of prestige that would have resulted from an open admission that American aircraft were roving over the Soviet Union at will, the Russians never made any form of protest; the first indication that they knew exactly what was happening came by way of an article in *Sovietskaya Aviatsiya*, which admitted that Russian intelligence officers were seriously worried about the threat to Soviet security posed by the American aircraft.

In 1959 and the early months of 1960, although the number of operational sorties was now somewhat reduced, the black-painted U-2s turned their attention to the IRBM and ICBM (Intermediate-Range and Intercontinental Ballistic Missile) sites which were springing up all over the Soviet Union. In April 1960 the US Central Intelligence Agency received information that the Russians had completed a very advanced missile site near Sverdlovsk, and a U-2 of the special CIA 10-10 Squadron was detailed to photograph it, together with the rocket research centre at Tyuratam and the air and naval bases at Archangelsk and Murmansk.

The U-2B selected for the mission was flown from Incirlik to Peshawar, in Pakistan, at the end of April. Its serial number was 566689, and it was not a favourite aircraft among the small band of CIA U-2 pilots, who had encountered fuel transfer problems while changing from one tank to another in the air as well as several other annoying snags in flying this particular machine. Nevertheless, it was the only U-2 that could be spared for this mission, so at 0620 local time on the morning of 1 May 1960 it took off from Peshawar and climbed out over northern Afghanistan on the first stage of a nine-hour, 2,800-mile flight over the Soviet Union that would terminate at nightfall on the NATO air base of Bodö, in northern Norway. The U-2's pilot was a civilian CIA employee, Francis Gary Powers.

By the time the U-2 crossed into Soviet territory it was flying at an altitude of 68,000 feet. Powers went up another couple of thousand feet, levelled out and switched over to the automatic pilot, noting casually that the outside air temperature was 60° C below zero.

Below the aircraft stretched an unbroken bank of cloud, not of particular significance from the reconnaissance point of view at this stage of the flight, for there was nothing much of interest on the surface. It made navigation just that little bit harder, for Powers – because of the strict conditions of radio silence imposed on him – was limited in the navigational aids at his disposal. Nevertheless, when the cloud layer finally ended he found himself more or less on track, south-east of the Aral Sea.

Looking down, Powers suddenly picked out a condensation trail, arrow-straight across the dark earth and on a reciprocal heading to his own. The aircraft that left it was travelling very fast, perhaps at supersonic speed, but it was a long way below and it quickly vanished. A few minutes later another contrail appeared, this time travelling in the same direction as the U-2, but this aircraft too remained far below and Powers eventually lost it.

Baikonur Cosmodrome – the space centre from which, a year later, Yuri Gagarin would blast off to become the first man in orbit – lay dead ahead, and although it was not a primary target on the U-2's itinerary it had been decided to include it anyway, as information brought back by previous U-2 flights had been disappointing. Powers therefore rolled his cameras as he passed over Baikonur before flying on towards Chelyabinsk.

The clouds had dispersed completely now, and the snow-capped Ural Mountains were clearly visible, running like a great jagged scar from south to north, cutting through green landscape on either side. Down there, it was spring. Suddenly, the U-2's nose pitched sharply upwards. Powers rapidly disengaged the autopilot and took over manual control, trimming the aircraft for level flight before engaging the autopilot again. The U-2 flew on for about ten minutes and then the nose pitched up again, leaving Powers no choice but to revert to manual control. The fact that he would have to pilot the aircraft manually for the rest of the sortie was by no means a disaster, but it would add considerably to his workload, and he would need all his concentration for the task of monitoring the U-2's reconnaissance systems.

At this point, Powers knew that he would have been quite justified in aborting the mission and turning back, for CIA U-2 pilots were briefed to take such action if anything at all went wrong with the programmed flight. By this time, however, Powers was about 1,300 miles deep into Russia and the weather conditions ahead of him were perfect. He decided to press on.

The U-2's next objective was Sverdlovsk, an important industrial centre which was of special interest to US Intelligence because of some curious domed structures, believed to be missile silos, which were reported to be under construction in the vicinity. So far, no U-2 flight had been made over the area.

Thirty miles south-east of Sverdlovsk, Powers made a turn to the left and settled down on a new heading that would take him over the strange installations and the south-west suburb of the town. He had now been airborne for four hours.

As he ran in towards the target at 70,000 feet, he suddenly detected an airfield which was not marked on his map, and he entered its position carefully. At that moment, he sensed rather than heard a dull explosion and a vivid orange light enveloped the aircraft, which lurched violently.

The U-2, in fact, had been near-missed by a rocket fired by an anti-aircraft battery on the outskirts of Sverdlovsk. Powers was unlucky; this battery was among the relatively few that had recently re-equipped with an improved version of the standard SA-2 surface-to-air missile, a weapon that gave the Soviet air defences a high 'kill' probability at altitudes of up to 90,000 feet.

Soviet missile technology had at last caught up with Lockheed's 'Black Lady'.

It seemed an age before the orange light died away. The U-2's right wing began to sink and Powers moved the control column over to the left, levelling the aircraft again. Then the U-2's nose dropped, and this time the controls failed to respond. An instant later, a fearful vibration shook the aircraft as both wings tore away. The weight of the engine dragged the tail down and Powers found himself lying on his back, staring up into the deep blue of the sky. The fuselage began to spin and the 'g' forces pinned him to his seat.

Powers knew that he had to get out, and quickly. He reached for the handle of his ejection seat, then a warning signal flashed through his brain and he paused.

The U-2's cockpit was small, the pilot sitting with his legs stretched out in a kind of tunnel beneath the instrument panel. The layout was much the same as that of a high-performance glider, but it meant that before he could eject, the U-2 pilot had to move his seat back on its rails and pull his legs clear of the panel. Powers pulled the lever that moved the seat, but it refused to budge. Quite simply, this meant that if he attempted to eject now, he would lose both legs a few inches above the knee as he blasted out of the cockpit.

The only other alternative was to bale out in the orthodox manner. A glance at the altimeter showed him that the U-2, still spinning wildly, was already below 35,000 feet and falling at an alarming rate. He pulled a knob and the transparent cockpit canopy whirled away. Almost instantly, the faceplate of his helmet frosted over. He unfastened his seat harness, then remembered that he was supposed to activate the U-2's destruct mechanism. If he had ejected this would have happened automatically, but now he had to throw a red-painted switch on the starboard side of the cockpit. He groped for it, unable to see because of his iced-up faceplate, but failed to locate it and decided to concentrate all his efforts on saving himself. He tried to lever himself out of the wildly gyrating cockpit, but something pulled him up sharply and there was a moment of panic before he remembered that he had not unclipped his oxygen lead. He tore it free, and the airflow whirled him clear of the plummeting fuselage.

Powers' parachute opened automatically at 15,000 feet and he landed in a ploughed field close to a Russian village. The rest is history. His subsequent interrogation and trial made worldwide headlines, and the U-2 incident effectively wrecked a major East-West summit conference which was scheduled to be held in Paris a fortnight later. Powers himself was sentenced to ten years' imprisonment in the Soviet Union, but after serving two years he was exchanged for the Russian spy Colonel Rudolf Abel.

After the loss of Powers, U-2 flights over the Soviet Union were suspended, but electronic reconnaissance operations around the periphery continued and it was not long before they claimed more lives. On 1 July 1960, while the Powers trial was still in progress, a Boeing RB-47 Stratojet reconnaissance aircraft was shot down over the Barents Sea – well outside Soviet air space – by an air-to-air missile fired from a MiG-19. Two of the four crew members parachuted to safety, were picked up by the Russians and later repatriated.

Several weeks before Powers and the U-2 burst into the world headlines, the prototype of the aircraft that was Russia's answer to the U-2 made its first flight. The Russians had not attempted to design an aircraft specifically for high-altitude reconnaissance; instead, they had taken the fuselage of one of the standard Soviet all-weather fighters, the Yakovlev Yak-25, and fitted it with an extended-span high aspect-ratio wing. In this way, a good performance at high altitude was made possible without a great deal of redesign; the Americans had followed the same technique a few years earlier, when they turned the Martin B-57 (a licence-built version of the British Canberra) into a high-altitude reconnaissance aircraft by giving it more power and extending its wingspan. At least two RB-57s, operating with the Chinese Nationalist Air Force, were shot down during surveillance flights over Red China in 1961.

The Russian aircraft, known as Mandrake under the NATO code-name system, became operational with several Soviet medium-range reconnaissance squadrons in April 1963. A single-seater with a wingspan of seventy feet, it was powered by two modified Klimov VK-9 engines and had an operational ceiling of 70,000 feet. In the late 1960s, aircraft of this type were known to have made short penetration flights into Greek and Turkish air space and over units of the US Sixth Fleet in the Mediterranean, and were probably also used to keep the Chinese nuclear production centres and testing grounds in Sinkiang under surveillance.

Meanwhile, the U-2s had been active again. In the summer of 1962 the Russians believed that they had found a chink in the defensive armour of the United States when they began to ship IRBMs, Ilyushin Il-28 jet bombers and surface-to-air missiles into Cuba. The Il-28s were intended to be flown by Cuban Air Force personnel, but the SA-2 anti-aircraft missiles and IRBMs were to be manned by Russians. Although the CIA were aware that modern Soviet weapons were arriving in Cuba, they did not know that these included strategic missiles until a U-2 aircraft revealed the secret on 14 October. Earlier reconnaissance flights, on 29 August and 5 September, had revealed nothing unusual except for a few vague patterns on the ground near Guanajay. They looked like earthworks, but it was impossible to identify them positively. Another reconnaissance flight was proposed on 4 October and approved five days later; the aircraft was all ready to go the next day, but poor weather intervened and the sortie was cancelled. The mission was finally accomplished, without incident, on Sunday 14 October, and from then until 26 October Cuba was kept under constant surveillance by U-2s and RF-101s of the USAF and by the RF-8A Crusaders of the US Navy's Light Photographic Squadron 26, which flew low-level missions over the island. The photographs they brought back clearly showed the presence of Soviet ballistic missiles on sites near San Cristobal, near the western tip of Cuba.

The story of the Cuban Missile Crisis, of the positive American reaction to the presence of the IRBMs and of their eventual withdrawal, is well known. What is not so well known is that on Saturday, 27 October, while the crisis was at its height, two separate incidents occurred thousands of miles apart, each involving U-2s and each escalating an already hyper-tense situation.

Early that morning, a U-2 was on a routine high-altitude reconnaissance mission over Cuba when it was shot down by a SA-2 missile, fired by a Russian crew. A few hours later a second U-2, genuinely engaged in a scientific flight to measure radiation in the upper atmosphere between Alaska and the North Pole, inadvertently strayed over cloud into Soviet air space over Russia's north-eastern tip. There was no question of this being a reconnaissance flight; the pilot had simply made a navigational error. But a few miles further south was the Red Army's important missile complex at Anadyr, and to the radar controllers of the IA-PVO – the Soviet Air Defence Force – the U-2's flight must have looked very much like a last-minute reconnaissance before an attack.

Within minutes, Russian fighters were climbing hard to intercept the American aircraft. By this time the U-2 pilot had realized his mistake and now swung round in a 45 degree turn over the coast, breaking radio silence to send out a call for help. A US controller in Alaska vectored a flight of F-104 Starfighters to the U-2's assistance, with orders to infringe Soviet air space if necessary. They made rendezvous with the U-2 over the Bering Strait and escorted it safely back to an Alaskan airfield. There was no sign of the Soviet fighters; they had failed to intercept.

1962 was not a good year for the U-2. In September and October, two of them were shot down over Communist China, one by a fighter and the other by an SA-2 missile. The following year, four U-2s were supplied to the Chinese Nationalist Air Force, and all of them were subsequently destroyed on operations. Yet another U-2 crashed in Cuba in October that year. In addition to losses on operations, at least seventeen U-2s were also accidentally destroyed. Despite their growing vulnerability, however, U-2s were used extensively over Vietnam, and also carried out surveillance over the Middle East during the Arab-Israeli wars of 1967 and 1973. About twenty were still in USAF service in 1980, and it was planned to use some of them – together with the U-2's ultra-secret successor, the Lockheed TR-1 – to monitor

Soviet missile tests under any future strategic arms limitation agreement.

In the meantime, the high cold war goes on, and continues to take its toll. The last known American casualties due to hostile action occurred on 14 April 1969, when North Korean jet fighters shot down an unarmed Lockheed EC-121 (a military version of the Super Constellation airliner) over the Sea of Japan. A US Navy aircraft, the EC-121, had been on Elint patrol from its base at Atsugi, Japan; all thirty-one men on board were killed. It was the biggest single loss of life sustained during electronic intelligence operations, and the American response was to activate a special naval task force, consisting of four aircraft carriers with an escort of cruisers and destroyers, to protect further Elint flights over international waters in that area.

Elint operations have cost the Russians aircraft and lives, too, but in their case the causes have been accidental. There is no known instance of a Soviet reconnaissance aircraft being fired on by NATO fighters. With the massive build-up of their naval strength in the 1960s, the Russians placed growing emphasis on maritime radar reconnaissance, and since then reconnaissance versions of Tu-16 'Badger', Mya-4 'Bison' and Tu-95 'Bear' bombers have ranged far afield over the world's oceans. Soviet aircraft regularly shadow NATO warships during exercises, and on one occasion a Tu-16 crashed into the sea while making a low run past a NATO task force in the north Atlantic.

Many of the Soviet Elint aircraft which patrol the crucial North Atlantic area – where a future conflict between East and West would probably be decided – are based on the Murmansk Peninsula, and the Russians are very touchy about any aircraft that approaches this sensitive area. On 21 April 1978 a South Korean Airlines Boeing 707 with 110 people on board made a serious navigational error and strayed into Russian air space; it was intercepted and attacked by a Soviet fighter, and only the skill of the pilot brought the aircraft down to a successful emergency landing on a frozen lake near Murmansk. Two of the occupants were killed and thirteen injured, the latest victims of the high cold war.

8 No Reply From 254

Major Klaus Lehnert lined up his aircraft on the main runway of Norvenich Air Base, eight miles south-west of Cologne, and settled himself firmly into his C-2 ejection seat, his practised eye scanning the instrument panel. Behind him, in the long fuselage, the idling General Electric J79 turbojet whined faintly. Satisfied that all was well, Lehnert pressed the R/T transmit button on his control column.

'Delta Alpha 254, take-off.'

The reply came back immediately from Norvenich tower. '254 clear take-off, wind zero four five at ten knots.'

From his vantage point in the tower, the aerodrome controller watched Lehnert's aircraft start its take-off roll, orange flames streaming from its tail pipe as the pilot cut in the afterburner. It climbed steeply away into the darkness, heading north-eastwards over Cologne. The large clock on the control tower wall indicated that it was 1709 hours; the date was 6 December 1965.

For the Norvenich controllers, it looked like being a busy evening. The weather had been bad during the day, but now it had cleared a little and night flying was in progress. Lehnert's sortie, for example, involved a night navigation exercise over North Germany, Holland and Belgium lasting about ninety minutes.

At the age of thirty-three, Klaus Lehnert was one of the Federal German Luftwaffe's most experienced jet pilots. He was a squadron commander with the 31st 'Boelcke' Fighter-Bomber Wing, a crack unit that bore the name of one of Germany's most famous fighter aces of World War I. Oswald Boelcke had met his end in 1916 while flying a flimsy Albatros biplane – an aircraft far removed from the supersonic jets which equipped the 31st Wing half a century later. They were Lockheed F-104G Starfighters, capable of attaining 90,000 feet in a zoom climb and of reaching a speed of 1,450 mph.

Of all the jet combat aircraft produced since 1945, the Lockheed Starfighter must surely rank as one of the most potent – and most controversial. The first model, the F-104A, entered service with the USAF Air Defense Command in 1958 as a pure interceptor; the first fighter-bomber version was the F-104C and this in turn led to the development of the F-104G, which was selected to equip several NATO air forces.

The F-104G, which was built by a consortium of European aircraft companies, was considerably heavier than previous models and, because of its multi-role task, embodied various modifications such as provision for underwing stores including rocket packs, bombs and fuel tanks. In certain configurations – at low speeds when heavily laden, for example – it could be tricky to handle and needed a firm touch. In the years following its introduction to the European NATO air forces its accident rate was high, particularly in service with the Luftwaffe, which received by far the largest number of F-104Gs produced, and as a consequence it acquired an undeserved reputation as a 'widow-maker'. The truth of the matter was that the F-104G was no more a killer than most other modern combat aircraft of its class, and in the hands of an experienced pilot, such as Klaus Lehnert, it was a formidable fighting machine.

The aircraft Lehnert was flying on this December evening in 1965 was a TF-104G, a two-seater trainer version, but on this occasion the rear cockpit was empty. The 31st Wing had two of them, and used them for routine continuation training and check flights.

At 1720, the Norvenich controller heard Lehnert call up on schedule, reporting his position over the Dortmund radio beacon.

'Norvenich, 254 over Dortmund at two zero, changing to – '

The pilot's voice was cut off in mid-sentence. The controller tried for a minute to contact him, then called Düsseldorf Radar and asked if they had contact with the Starfighter. After a delay of a few seconds, Düsseldorf confirmed that they had radar contact with the aircraft; it was heading almost due north.

The controller at Norvenich felt a sudden surge of alarm. Lehnert should have altered course over Dortmund, heading west. It was not like an experienced pilot such as Major Lehnert to make an elementary mistake; something was clearly wrong.

After repeated attempts to contact the Starfighter, without any success, the Norvenich controller, fearing the worst, issued a general alert. Soon afterwards, radar stations in northern Germany reported that DA 254 was speeding out over the coast near Bremerhaven at 30,000 feet, following an arrow-straight course towards the north.

At Norvenich, anxiety rose to fever-pitch. Senior officers of the 31st Wing, alerted by the controller, converged on the tower to keep track of events as reports on the TF-104G's progress continued to come in from NATO radar units. The aircraft was still holding a steady course at 30,000 feet, and it began to look as though some misfortune had overcome the pilot. Whatever the reason, an uncontrolled bomb was now hurtling across Europe at a height of six miles, and no one knew where it might plunge to earth with devastating effect. The only certain thing was that Lehnert had taken off with a full load of fuel, which meant that the Starfighter could fly for over 1,200 miles. If it continued on its present course, its fuel would run out somewhere over northern Norway—but there was an even more frightening possibility: if the hurtling fighter veered eastwards, without losing altitude, it would come down somewhere along an arc running west of Moscow.

At 1750, radar reports indicated that the Starfighter had crossed into Danish territory and, although its altitude remained a steady 30,000 feet, it had altered course slightly to 010 degrees, a little to the east of north. By this time the Danish Air Defence Command had been warned of the TF-104G's rogue flight, and at 1800 two Danish Air Force F-100 Super Sabres took off from Skrydstrup to carry out a visual inspection of the German aircraft.

The Danish pilots formated on either side of the Starfighter and made several attempts to contact Lehnert by radio, but there was no answer. Moving in as closely as they dared, they surveyed the TF-104G's cockpit in the moonlight and reported that Lehnert appeared to be either dead or unconscious, his head slumped forward. The Danish fighters followed the Starfighter until 1805, when it crossed the cloud-shrouded coast of north Denmark and headed out over the Skagerrak.

By this time a minute-by-minute plot of the Starfighter's flight had been set up in the operations room at Norvenich. At 1820, a Norwegian tracking radar reported that it was passing over Fredrikstad, still heading 010 degrees at 30,000 feet, above cloud. As details of its course and speed were passed to Norvenich, Luftwaffe experts calculated exactly where it would crash, assuming that it flew on until its fuel was exhausted.

At 1940 hours, give or take a few seconds, the Starfighter would explode like a bomb somewhere within the perimeter of Narvik, a town of 13,000 inhabitants inside the Arctic Circle.

By 1830, it was apparent that the runaway Starfighter's career would take it across the western fringe of Swedish territory, so the Swedish Air Force was alerted. A few minutes later, the Swedes confirmed that the TF-104G had entered their airspace near the little town of Fulu Fjallet and was heading out over the mountainous, lake-studded region of western Jämtland. The risk of damage to life or property was small if the jet came down here; nevertheless, the Swedish Air Force 'scrambled' a pair of Saab J-35 Draken fighters to keep track of the German aircraft's progress. Before they could make contact, however, the Starfighter had re-entered Norwegian air space, so they abandoned the chase and returned to their base.

At 1855, the alarm bell shrilled in the readiness hut of the Royal Norwegian Air Force's No. 331 (Fighter) Squadron at Bödö airfield, fifty miles inside the Arctic Circle. The two pilots on QRA – Quick Reaction Alert – tossed aside the magazines they had been reading and grabbed their helmets, racing outside to their F-100 Super Sabre fighters which were parked in nearby blast pens. For both men, this was a routine drill; 'scramble' calls at a moment's notice were part of everyday life at Bödö, where pairs of fighters were required to take off several times a week to investigate suspicious aircraft. The latter were usually Soviet reconnaissance aircraft, en route from their bases on the Murmansk Peninsula into the north Atlantic, and the NATO fighters would ensure that they stayed clear of Norwegian air space. The routes followed by the Russian aircraft were well known, and later, as they passed north of the Shetland Islands, surveillance would be taken over by Lightning fighters of the Royal Air Force.

On this occasion, however, things were different. As the two pilots – Captain Magne Uv and his wingman, Sergeant Marthinsen – started their engines and began to roll forward for take-off, they were briefed over the R/T by the Bödö fighter controller. The orders passed to them were quite specific; they were to shadow the Starfighter and try to contact its pilot over the radio – and, if the German fighter showed signs of coming down in a populated area, they were to destroy it.

The two Super Sabres thundered down Bödö's active runway at 1900 hours and pulled up in a battle climb, their afterburners glowing as they raced through the cloud layer on a south-easterly heading to intercept the runaway Starfighter. They had no difficulty in locating it, for it was leaving a long condensation trail that shone eerily in the light of the moon.

The Starfighter was flying at no more than 450 knots and the Super Sabres curved round astern of it, spreading out to formate on either wing. Magne Uv used his radio navaids to check his position; the town of Mosjoen was far below, hidden under its blanket of cloud. A quick mental calculation told the captain that, according to Luftwaffe estimates, the TF-104G had fuel for another twenty-five minutes' flying. He checked the time: it was now 1915 hours.

Captain Uv flicked a switch, arming the Super Sabre's four 20-millimetre M.39 cannon, and ordered Sergeant Marthinsen to do the same. Then he carefully edged his aircraft closer and looked across into the Starfighter's cockpit.

'My first impression,' he said later, 'was that there was no

93

pilot in there. Then I saw his white helmet flash in the moonlight. He was sitting in a hunched-forward position, his chin sunk on his chest. I tried to make radio contact with him on various frequencies, using both his aircraft call-sign and his name, but there was no response. He never made the slightest movement. I knew that his aircraft would soon run out of fuel; it was pretty harrowing, sitting there alongside him and not being able to do a thing to help him.'

The strange formation sped on, heading deeper into the Arctic night, and as the minutes went by Magne Uv knew that soon he would have to follow his orders and shoot down the Starfighter. It was a grim decision to have to take, for there was no way of knowing whether Lehnert was dead or merely unconscious.

In Narvik, the air-raid sirens were going full blast. The last time they had sounded the warning of an approaching German aircraft had been in 1940, under vastly different circumstances. The town's fire brigade was standing by and police cars cruised through the streets, their loud-hailers warning people to take shelter. Most of the townsfolk thought it was some sort of civil defence exercise and took no notice.

With the predicted end of Lehnert's flight approaching fast, and Narvik just over the horizon, Captain Uv knew that he dared delay no longer. Ordering his wingman to get clear, he throttled back slightly and dropped astern of the Starfighter, ready to make a careful firing pass.

At that moment, the Starfighter's engine stopped, starved of fuel. Magne Uv saw the red glow of the jet exhaust fade away. Powerless now, the TF-104G lost height rapidly, and a minute later it disappeared in the clouds below. The two Norwegians followed it as it plummeted earthwards, and broke through the overcast just in time to see the flash as the German fighter impacted. It had struck a ridge near Ankenes, just three miles short of Narvik. The time was exactly 1942.

The Luftwaffe specialists had been correct to within seconds in their forecast of when the fighter's fuel would be exhausted. Later, they established that if the Starfighter had been flying only twenty feet higher, it would have missed the ridge altogether and its trajectory would have caused it to impact somewhere in Narvik, as they had feared.

The wreckage of the Starfighter was recovered, together with Lehnert's body, and Luftwaffe technical staff began a searching investigation to determine what had caused the accident. Two weeks later, they were still unable to agree on a likely cause. Then, from the Royal Netherlands Air Force, came a report that one of their Starfighters had been lost under almost carbon copy circumstances. The pilot, Major Heitmeiler, had taken off on a routine night exercise and contact had been lost with him shortly afterwards, although radar stations tracked his fighter as it headed out over the North Sea. It was intercepted by a Norwegian Air Force Starfighter, whose pilot reported that Heitmeiler – just like Lehnert – was slumped forward in his seat and appeared to be either dead or deeply unconscious. After a 25-minute flight the Dutch Starfighter plunged into the sea off Kristiansund and broke up. The pilot's body was later recovered, and examinations showed that the accident had been due to a single cause : anoxia. At some stage, miles above the earth, his oxygen supply had failed, inducing a numbing state of lethargy leading to unconsciousness. So, like Klaus Lehnert, he had flown on in an aircraft that had become a speeding metal coffin, dead at the controls long before the Starfighter went into its last long dive.

9 Runaway Missile

Like a great, ungainly bird, far removed from its true element, its long, swept wings drooping under the combined weight of tons of fuel and the eight Pratt and Whitney turbojets slung in pods underneath them, the mighty Boeing B-52 Stratofortress taxied slowly around the perimeter track of Biggs Air Force Base near El Paso, Texas.

In the B-52's rear turret, isolated from the rest of the crew by 160 feet of slender fuselage, Sergeant Ray Singleton, the tail gunner, had little to do but glance at the parked B-52s of the 95th Bomb Wing as his own aircraft rolled past them. Over the intercom, he could hear the other seven crew members busy with their pre-flight checks. For the time being, Singleton could afford to relax; his turn to be vigilant would come later, seven miles above the New Mexico desert, far beyond the layer of broken cloud that was spreading slowly across the sky.

Not for the first time, Singleton felt intensely proud to be part of a first-rate fighting team. For Singleton and his crew, and the mighty bomber that carried them, were only small cogs in the giant machine of the United States Air Force's Strategic Air Command. Dispersed on bases throughout the United States, or on detachment overseas, were five hundred and forty-nine more B-52s grouped in thirty-two Bomb Wings. Together – and not forgetting the medium jet bombers of the RAF's V-Force – they formed the free world's nuclear deterrent. In time of war, every one of those Bomb Wings could have their aircraft off the ground in minutes, fanning out as they climbed to minimize the effects of nuclear blast in case their bases were about to come under sudden attack. Then they would spear towards their targets somewhere deep in the heart of the Soviet Union, their bellies laden with enough thermonuclear death to wipe out an entire continent. Part of the B-52 force was always airborne, ready to retaliate instantly if the West came under surprise attack.

Despite their doomsday role, the men of Strategic Air Command were always conscious that their task was to prevent war, not to start it. Inside every SAC crew-room, a large sign proclaimed: 'Peace Is Our Profession'. And that just about summed it up. If SAC and the other nuclear strike forces of the free world ever ceased to deter a potential aggressor, then the world would be free no longer.

The B-52, SAC's formidable spearhead, was the most remarkable strategic bomber ever built. It traced its ancestry back to World War II and the piston-engined Boeing B-29 Superfortress, the aircraft that enabled the Americans to conduct a shattering long-range bombing offensive against Japan in 1945, culminating in the dropping of atomic bombs on Hiroshima and Nagasaki. In September 1945, only days after the end of the war, the Boeing aircraft company began design work on a new jet bomber to replace the B-29. The new aircraft, which emerged as the B-47 Stratojet, was a radical departure from conventional design, featuring a thin, flexible swept wing – based on wartime German research data – which carried six turbojets in underwing pods. A thousand Stratojets had been delivered to the USAF by the end of 1954, and the bulk of SAC's bomber wings were equipped with the type until 1955, when the B-52 began to enter service.

The B-52, which first flew in 1951, was much larger and heavier than the B-47. The first production version, the B-52B – the model that equipped the 95th Bomb Wing – weighed close on 180 tons fully laden. Its mighty wings spanned 185 feet, and under the power of its eight Pratt and Whitney J57 turbojets it could climb to 55,000 feet, reach a speed of over 630 mph and fly 9,000 miles without refuelling.

The B-52 was thus the 'big stick' of America's nuclear deterrent, filling the dangerous gap that existed until nuclear submarines and intercontinental ballistic missiles were available in sufficient numbers to take over the deterrent role. And during those dangerous years of the late 1950s and early 1960s SAC's efficiency depended on one factor above all others: constant, rigorous training, so that each crew, each squadron, each wing became welded together like a single entity, supremely confident in its ability to carry out its mission.

That was why, on this morning of 7 April 1961, Singleton's B-52 was taxi-ing out towards the end of the runway at Biggs Air Force Base. The crew had gone through their flight plan during a lengthy briefing session the day before; it involved flying a series of dog-leg courses across half the North American continent, locating and bombing a series of selected targets from high altitude with the aid of radar. The bombing, of course, would be simulated, for on training flights the B-52's huge bomb-bay was empty. There was a strong element of competition involved, too, for in the course of an air exercise lasting several days the SAC crew that emerged with the best navigation and simulated bombing results would receive a coveted trophy for their Wing.

There would also be opposition. Somewhere over New Mexico, the B-52 was scheduled to be intercepted by 'enemy' fighters. They would, in fact, be aircraft of the Air National Guard, the territorial force raised by each US state. Although composed mainly of part-time reserve personnel, the ANG flew modern aircraft and formed an important operational element of the USAF. In times of crisis, such as the Korean War, ANG units were brought into active service, flying combat alongside regular USAF squadrons. Like SAC, their efficiency and operational readiness depended on the highest possible level of training.

The B-52 turned on to the main runway, and Ray Singleton, strapped in his turret at the base of the bomber's forty-foot-high tail-fin, felt the surge of acceleration as the engines opened up to full power. The runway blurred underneath him, then fell away as the aircraft commander, Captain Don Blodgett, lifted the big bird cleanly away. Streams of black smoke from the B-52's thundering engines swept past Singleton's turret as the bomber climbed steeply towards the overcast.

The intercom chatter continued as the crew went on with their flight checks. Every member of the crew, officers and enlisted men alike, knew one another as intimately as if they had been brought up together. In the air, rank was of secondary importance. The main thing was teamwork, with each man knowing precisely what he had to do. Mentally, Singleton ticked off the names of the crew. Seated next to Blodgett, in the B-52's roomy cockpit, was the co-pilot, Captain Ray Obel. Behind them were the two navigators, Captain Peter Gineris and Captain Steve Carter. The latter was lucky to be alive; only the year before, he had been the sole survivor of a B-47 which had plunged into the sea off the Azores. Then came the air warfare officer, Captain George Jackson, and the air electronics officer, Second Lieutenant Glen Bair. Last, but far from least, was Sergeant Manuel Mieras, the crew chief, whose task was to check out the B-52's systems, supervise ground handling and ensure that the whole machine was completely serviceable and airworthy before each flight. He knew the giant bomber inside out.

The B-52 broke through the overcast and climbed to its operational height of 36,000 feet, the brilliant sunshine glinting on its light grey upper surfaces. The bomber's underside was painted white to give protection from the flash of her thermonuclear weapons, if ever she had to fly her last doomsday mission. On her nose, under the cockpit, was painted the name *Ciudad Juarez*, after El Paso's sister town just across the border in Mexico.

Seven miles up in the sky the bomber plunged on through the dazzling, rarefied air at a speed of nearly ten miles a minute, dragging a broad white vapour trail in her wake. Two hours later she reached the first turning-point of the exercise, right on time. The navigators were spot on, as usual, and their efforts drew a brief word of praise from Blodgett. With his thumb and index finger, he turned the knob of the autopilot control slightly and brought the massive aircraft round in a gentle turn, heading for the next target, and called up Ray Singleton as he did so.

'Tail gunner, this is AC.'

'AC, this is tail gunner, go ahead.'

'Ray, those National Guard planes are scheduled to make some passes at us pretty soon. Keep your eyes open for them.'

'Roger, sir.'

Singleton became alert at once, peering beyond the barrels of his twin 20-millimetre cannon, searching the burning expanse of sky for a glimpse of tell-tale contrails. In time of war, the keenness of his eyes might mean the difference between life and death for the eight men on board the B-52.

Admittedly, his position was equipped with airborne warning radar, but his eyes were the decisive factor in determining whether an approaching aircraft was hostile or friendly.

Still many miles away, high over the New Mexico desert, a pair of F-100 Super Sabres of the Air National Guard's 188th Fighter Interceptor Squadron from Kirtland Air Force Base, near Albuquerque, swung round in a wide circle, cruising almost lazily to conserve fuel while they awaited instructions from 'Blush First', the local Ground Controlled Intercept Station. The pilot of the leading aircraft was First Lieutenant James 'Sock' Van Sycoc, a sturdy, dark-haired regular USAF officer with ten years service and 1,900 hours' flying time behind him, 1,000 of them on Super Sabres. His wingman was a National Guard pilot, Captain Dale Dodd.

The North American F-100 was a potent interceptor. Born during the years of the Korean War, it incorporated many of the lessons learned by the pilots of its predecessor, the famous F-86 Sabre, in combat against Russian-built MiG-15 jets over the Yalu River. The first operational jet aircraft in the world capable of exceeding the speed of sound in level flight, the F-100 later established several world air speed records. It carried a powerful armament of four 20-millimetre cannon in the nose, and two Sidewinder heat-seeking air-to-air missiles on pylons under its wings.

The F-100s flown by Van Sycoc and Dodd were both armed and ready for combat. Although this was a training flight, the pilots might have to intercept an unidentified aircraft; and if that aircraft turned out to be hostile, they would have to shoot it down.

Crackling over Van Sycoc's headphones, the voice of the GCI controller came up with the information on the altitude of the approaching B-52, and the course the fighters would have to steer to intercept it. Both pilots now carried out a vital part of the procedure: the armament safety check. Their gloved hands moved over the console positioned at the side of the instrument-packed cockpit, checking a battery of switches and circuit breakers. Everything was on 'safe', which meant that neither the cannon nor the Sidewinders could be fired. Van Sycoc and Dodd both confirmed this to the GCI controller.

With their weapons now inert the F-100s streaked towards their target, sliding effortlessly past Mach 1 as the pilots opened the throttles. A few moments later, a shimmering blip appeared on Van Sycoc's radar screen: the B-52. Van Sycoc called 'Tally ho' over the radio and the two F-100s formed up for a simulated missile attack, curving in sharply and reducing speed once more, their wings glittering in the harsh sunlight. In the B-52's cockpit, Captain Ray Obel caught sight of them as they flashed past, rolling into a turn for a second attack. From his position in the tail turret, Ray Singleton, who had alerted the crew of the fighters' approach, watched fascinated as the Super Sabres bored in again and again, making simulated cannon-firing passes.

Van Sycoc glanced at his fuel gauges, and called up Dodd.

'Okay,' he said. 'One more run, and then we'll go home.'

The fighters closed in for another simulated missile pass, lining up astern of the B-52 and streaking over the swirling contrail. In a real attack, the missiles would home in on the hot exhaust gases pouring from the bomber's engines. Van Sycoc's F-100, in the lead, rapidly overhauled the Stratofortress. The pilot watched the bomber's big tail and long, flexing wings loom bigger and bigger in his sights.

Suddenly, his aircraft seemed to jerk slightly. Something leaped ahead of it and streaked towards the bomber – a glowing thing, dragging a fiery trail.

Van Sycoc's heart leaped into his mouth. Frantically, he pressed the transmit button and yelled a warning over the radio.

'Look out – one of my missiles has fired!'

It was too late. With dreadful, unerring accuracy, the Sidewinder sped straight towards its target, the hot, pulsing gases churning out behind a pair of the B-52's engines, slung in their pod under the huge port wing. There was a vivid orange flash, a gush of black smoke, and the stricken B-52 reared up and rolled viciously to the left, spewing chunks of burning metal.

In the Stratofortress's cockpit, Blodgett and Obel heard Van Sycoc's frantic warning shout. A second later, they were crushed into their seats as the great bomber swung crazily over on its wingtip. For a few moments Blodgett wrestled with the controls, helplessly, as the B-52 twisted out of the sky. Then, quickly ordering the rest of the crew to bale out, he pulled the handles of his ejection seat and felt himself blasted out into space.

In the rear turret, Ray Singleton had been bewildered by the sheer speed of the disaster. He had caught a brief glimpse of the Sidewinder's black smoke trail, and had been stunned by the numbing shock of the impact. Dimly, he heard Blodgett order the crew to abandon the aircraft. He jettisoned his turret, unfastened his seat harness and tumbled out into the slipstream – straight into the roaring, agonizing river of flame that poured back in the bomber's wake. He hung there for what seemed an eternity, suspended in the searing inferno, and then mercifully he was falling away, dropping through the clean, freezing sky.

Up above, the two fighter pilots, paralysed with horror, watched as the shattered remains of the eight-million-dollar B-52 plunged into the cloud layer below. They could see no sign of any parachutes. Transmitting emergency signals, Van Sycoc and Dodd let down cautiously into the swirling vapour. They had to be careful, for somewhere in all this murk was the 11,400-foot peak of Mount Taylor. It was no use; they couldn't see a thing. The clouds extended right down to 6,000 feet, almost to the level of the high plateau of the New Mexican desert. Cramming on power, the pilots lifted their Super Sabres out of the cottonwool and set course for Kirtland Air Force Base.

Kirtland, alerted by Van Sycoc's distress call, was a hive of activity. One of the biggest USAF bases, it handled a large amount of air traffic, both military and civilian. Consequently, its search and rescue facilities were among the best to be found anywhere. As the two F-100s landed, four rescue helicopters were preparing to take off, the clatter of their rotors adding to the din made by three T-33 jet trainers which were just climbing away from the runway to take part in the search.

The wreckage of the B-52 lay 9,000 feet high on the slopes of Mount Taylor. Because the fighter pilots had reported seeing no parachutes, the rescuers who toiled towards it did not entertain much hope that there would be any survivors. To make matters worse, a cold front was moving in and visibility was getting steadily worse as the rescue aircraft roared back and forth over the craggy rocks.

Suddenly, within five hours of the tragedy, came the electrifying news that a survivor had been sighted. It was Don Blodgett. His pelvis was fractured and he was unable to move. He was spotted by the pilot of a T-33 jet, who guided a Kaman H-43 rescue helicopter to his position. A few minutes later, the same jet pilot sighted a second survivor: Ray Singleton. The tail gunner was badly burned about the face as a result of his fall through the flames that streamed from the shattered bomber.

The helicopter was just climbing away, with Blodgett and Singleton safely on board, when the latter shouted that he had seen another parachute. The Kaman descended again, and this time found Captain George Jackson, the air warfare officer. His back was broken. Gently, the rescuers lifted him into the helicopter, which took off and headed back to Kirtland at top speed. It was almost incredible that the three injured men had fallen so close together, and the fact probably saved their lives. Not long after they were picked up the temperature dropped almost to zero and a raging storm blasted over the crash area, accompanied by freezing 70-mph winds. Blodgett and Jackson, incapacitated by their injuries, would almost certainly have succumbed to exposure.

All that night and the next day the storm howled, bringing the rescue operation to a standstill. The helicopter pilots, with great courage and disregard for their own safety, went on flying as long as they could, but before long even take-off became impossible. Only one ground party managed to battle its way up Mount Taylor and reached the place where the wreckage of the B-52 lay, strewn in a smoking, blackened mass around a huge crater.

Beneath that heap of charred and twisted metal lay the bodies of the air electronics officer, Glen Bair, and the two navigators, Pete Gineris and Steve Carter. Death, which Carter had cheated by a hair's breadth in the Atlantic only months earlier, had claimed him in the end.

On 9 April, after the storm had blown itself out, the flash of a hand mirror brought a rescuer to yet another of the survivors. It was the crew chief, Sergeant Manuel Mieras. When the aircraft broke up, he had suddenly found himself hanging in space under his parachute. He had no idea how he had got clear of the wreckage. He broke a leg on landing, but fashioned a makeshift crutch from a tree branch and managed to hobble as far as a shepherd's hut, where he had sheltered from the elements until the rescue aircraft flew overhead.

It was a flashing mirror, too, that drew the searchers to the co-pilot, Captain Ray Obel. He was suffering from shock; his parachute, which should not have opened until he reached 10,000 feet, had actually deployed twenty thousand feet higher up with a terrific jolt, and Obel had suffered badly from the cold during his long descent. Adding to his ordeal, he had landed right in the middle of a cactus patch. After he had picked dozens of painful spines from his face and hands, he spent the next day and night wrapped in his parachute, with his inflatable life-raft pulled over him for shelter.

Three men had died; five others were saved. And now came the searching inquiry : why had Van Sycoc's missile fired?

It was quickly established that the pilot had been in no way to blame, and that all the proper safeguards against an accidental launch had been meticulously carried out. One thing above all puzzled the investigators; both Sidewinders had been carried under one wing of Van Sycoc's F-100, the pylon under the other wing having been occupied by a fuel tank, and for aerodynamic reasons the outer missile could only be fired after the inner one.

Yet it was the outer Sidewinder that had destroyed the B-52 – a technical impossibility.

Only when the missile firing circuits were stripped down did the amazing answer come to light. A tiny blot of moisture in the system had been to blame. In a million-to-one chance, an impulse from the F-100's electrical system had passed through the blot into the missile firing circuit. The Sidewinder had launched itself, sped mindlessly to its target – and a giant bomber had gone down in flames.

10 Ordeal in the Berlin Corridor

For television personality Hughie Green, flying was second nature. He had been in and out of aircraft for more than twenty years, ever since his days as a pilot with the Royal Canadian Air Force during World War II, and the types he had flown ranged from light single-engined trainers to four-engined heavy bombers.

Compared to some of them, the little twin-engined Cessna 310 executive aircraft – in whose comfortable, upholstered cockpit he now sat – was child's play. The Cessna cruised at just over 200 miles per hour and Green used it a lot to make flights around Europe. It saved a lot of time and frustration, and Green – star of television shows such as 'Double Your Money' and 'Opportunity Knocks' – found himself able to relax completely once he was in the air, where he felt quite at home.

Green went through the pre-take-off checks meticulously, his practised eye scanning the instrument panel, watching pressures, temperatures and rpm, holding the Cessna on the brakes as he opened the throttles and checked each engine for magneto drop. Pulling the throttles back to idle once more, he tested the controls for full and free movement. Everything worked perfectly. There was nothing left to do now but call the control tower and request take-off clearance.

It was the morning of 1 April 1963. In a few moments, Green would lift the Cessna – call-sign 'Golf Alpha Romeo Oscar Kilo' – away from the active runway of Stuttgart Airport, West Germany, en route to Berlin, where he was to give a show for

Royal Air Force personnel. Next to him in the six-seater aircraft sat 54-year-old Cliff Luxton, the co-pilot, and in one of the seats behind was Jim Preston, a journalist.

The journey called for some precise navigation, for much of the flight had to be made over Soviet-controlled East German territory by way of the Frankfurt-Berlin air corridor, one of three fifteen-mile-wide invisible roads in the sky that led to the airfields of the divided city. Any aircraft wishing to use the corridors had to adhere strictly to predetermined tracks and altitudes, and special clearances had to be obtained before a flight commenced. If an aircraft strayed outside the limits of the corridor, it would be intercepted by Soviet fighters and compelled to land. If the crew failed to obey instructions, they risked being shot down.

This had been the fate of several aircraft in the past, and now, with East-West tension at a new peak – it was less than two years since the building of the Berlin Wall, and only a matter of months since the Cuban missile crisis, which had brought the world to the brink of war – Green and Luxton were taking no chances.

Before the Cessna left England, Cliff Luxton – who had undertaken to handle all the necessary navigational and radio procedures – had attended a briefing at the Ministry of Aviation Briefing Unit at Ruislip, and had come away with a dossier full of route information, radio frequencies and visual signals to be used in the event of interception. A couple of days later, he had received confirmation from the Ministry that the flight had been cleared by the appropriate authorities. Neither he nor Hughie Green expected any problems.

Having completed his take-off checks, Green nodded to Luxton, who called up Stuttgart tower, requesting airways clearance followed by permission to take off. The controller came back immediately:

'Oscar Kilo is cleared to Berlin Gatow via Airways Green three-one and Red one-zero, joining airways at Frankfurt, Flight level nine-five. You are cleared for immediate take-off; the surface wind is two-three-zero degrees, fifteen knots.'

Luxton acknowledged and Green turned on to the runway, lining up the Cessna and opening the throttle smoothly. Moments later, he lifted the blue-and-white machine off the ground and turned on to a heading of 346 degrees, climbing steadily and concentrating on his instruments as the Cessna nosed up into the overcast. At 4,000 feet they burst through into brilliant sunshine and Green continued the climb until they reached 9,500 feet, when he levelled out. The little aircraft cruised on serenely at 200 mph, with the sky to itself, flying from radio beacon to radio beacon, the instruments telling the pilot and navigator when they were directly overhead each one. Over Lauffen, Luxton switched radio frequencies, calling Frankfurt Control and passing the details of their route. He was informed that Frankfurt Control had the Cessna's flight plan, and that the aircraft was cleared to proceed to Fulda radio beacon.

Twenty years earlier, Fulda Beacon had been one of the favourite assembly points for German night-fighters, waiting to strike at the great Allied bomber streams that were thundering towards Berlin. Now, a vastly improved beacon still served as a pointer to the former capital. Green turned on to a new heading of 055 degrees, following Airway Red 10 now, and the Cessna's radio equipment soon indicated that the aircraft was over Fulda. Luxton contacted Frankfurt again and heard the controller clear the Cessna to the beacon at Mansbach, the gateway to the southern air corridor.

Luxton bade the controller good-day and switched to Berlin Control. The voice that replied over the radio was rich, deep and American, somehow warming in its friendliness after the clipped and precise tones of the Frankfurt controller. The American confirmed that the Cessna was following the centre-line of the corridor, as planned, and that it was cleared to proceed to Gatow Airfield, in the British Zone of Berlin, at 9,500 feet. Green and Luxton glanced at one another, grinning and relaxing. It was pleasantly warm in the cockpit, with the sun beating down out of a limitless blue sky. Thousands of feet below, the unbroken cloud layer shone brilliantly white.

They had been flying for several minutes when the voice of the

American controller, urgent now, burst suddenly over the radio.

'Oscar Kilo, fast unidentified aircraft approaching you from five o'clock.'

Luxton, in the right-hand seat, twisted round to look down and to the rear, past the trailing edge of the Cessna's starboard wing. At first he could see nothing – and then, abruptly, a black dot popped out of the cloud layer, hurtling at high speed straight towards them. It came at them like a bullet and Luxton lost sight of it behind the tail. Moments later it reappeared, climbing steeply in front of the Cessna's nose and rocking its wings.

There was no doubt about its identity. Short, stubby delta wings, swept tail surfaces, a stovepipe-like fuselage, all added up to one of the Soviet's Air Force's most potent interceptors, the supersonic MiG-21.

The MiG came out of its climb, turned sharply to the right and then curved round for another fast run past the Cessna, rocking its wings once more. Luxton recognized the signal; it meant 'follow me and land'.

Luxton pressed the R/T button, quickly telling the Berlin Controller what was happening. The controller confirmed that he was watching the whole business on his radar screen, and also confirmed that the Cessna was still on the corridor centre-line. There was no apparent reason why the Soviet fighter should have been sent up to intercept it.

The Russian pilot, however, clearly meant business. He made a third pass, this time streaking so close past the Cessna that his slipstream buffeted the little aircraft.

Luxton kept an eye on the Russian fighter while Green concentrated on holding the Cessna on course. The MiG was curving round from the right-hand side again, but this time there was a difference; the Russian had lowered his undercarriage and flaps to reduce the fighter's speed. Wobbling slightly, its nose well up as it teetered a few knots above stalling speed, the MiG came alongside the Cessna and the occupants had a clear view of the masked, helmeted pilot, his face turned towards them. As they watched, he raised a hand, jabbing earthwards with his index finger, and then pointed over his shoulder towards the Soviet zone. There could be no mistaking the message he wished to convey.

Green stuck doggedly to his course. He had no wish to be forced to land on some Russian airfield; no one in the Cessna could speak Russian, neither he nor Luxton had any knowledge of Soviet approach and landing procedures, and since there were several cameras on board the aircraft it was all too probable that they would be accused of spying. In another few minutes they would reach Berlin, and safety – if they could keep the Russian fighter at bay for that long.

The Russian pilot abruptly whipped up his landing gear and crammed on power, pulling ahead of the Cessna and turning away. Green lost sight of him, but a minute later Luxton reported that he was coming in again, about five hundred yards astern and off to the right. He had hardly finished speaking when orange flashes lit up the MiG's nose and smoky tracer trails streamed past the Cessna's starboard wingtip.

Striving to keep his voice calm, Luxton called up Berlin Control and reported that the Russian fighter had opened fire. He was told to change frequency to Berlin Military Control, who informed him that the Cessna's clearance still held good and that the light aircraft was still on the centre-line of the corridor.

The MiG, meanwhile, had shot past and was coming in for another run. Closing in fast, the Russian opened fire and this time his cannon shells passed only feet from the Cessna's starboard wingtip fuel tank. An instant later, Green was fighting to retain control as the fighter whistled past; the Russian pilot was deliberately slicing his wingtip under that of the Cessna, obviously trying to use his high-speed airflow to turn the light aircraft upside down.

A lesser pilot might have lost control, but Green righted the aircraft and waited for the Russian's next move. At that moment, Berlin Military Control came on the air again :

' Oscar Kilo, we have radar contact with another aircraft, coming up fast from nine o'clock.'

Green peered out to his left, and a moment later saw the

newcomer shoot up out of the cloud like a rocket. It was much larger than the MiG, with sharply swept wings and twin jet engines. He identified it as a Yakovlev Yak-25. Now they had a real problem, for the Yak-25, which was heavily armed with cannon and air-to-air missiles, was an all-weather fighter. That meant that even if they tried to escape into the cloud, the Yak could follow them down and open fire with the aid of its airborne interception radar.

The Yak continued its climb, arrowing up into the sky for thousands of feet above the Cessna. Then it turned, hurtling down on the very edge of the speed of sound. Misty shock waves danced over its wings as it sped in front of Green's aircraft, and this time not even Green's expertise could bring them through the fearsome turbulence. The shock waves struck the aircraft with a terrific jolt and the Cessna rolled uncontrollably to the right until it was almost on its back. Green pushed the control column hard over in the opposite direction and the aircraft responded slowly, wallowing back into level flight once more.

Then the starboard engine stopped, starved of fuel, and they began to lose height. Green juggled with the ignition and managed to restart the motor, but by that time they were down to 7,500 feet. Luxton made another hurried call to Berlin Military Control, and was told that they were cleared to proceed to Berlin at their new altitude. They were, however, to use their own discretion with regard to signals from the Russian aircraft.

Green and Luxton exchanged significant glances. With the odds stacked formidably against them, they had two alternatives. Either they could follow the Russians – or they could take the fearful risk of making a run for it.

The MiG-21 was approaching from astern again, the Russian pilot intent on manoeuvring his wingtip under the Cessna's, but this time Green was ready for him. As the MiG came racing up, slightly off to one side, Green suddenly lowered his undercarriage and pulled off all the power. The Russian pilot, taken completely by surprise, shot past at high speed and pulled up in a steep climb.

The Soviet pilot now changed his tactics. Turning at the top of his climb, he entered a steep dive, pulling out and spearing head-on towards the Cessna. At the very last moment when a collision seemed inevitable, the Russian pulled up sharply and screamed over the top of the Cessna, battering it with shock waves again. The MiG pilot repeated the manoeuvre twice more; on the third run he approached from in front and a little to one side, and Green, remembering his wartime training, hauled the Cessna round to meet the fighter head-on. His sudden action seemed to unnerve the Soviet pilot, who twisted away violently. The fighter shuddered and went into a high-speed stall, then spun down towards the cloud layer.

There was no time for Green to congratulate himself, for now the Yak-25, which had been circling overhead, came screaming down once more to lay its wake of turbulence across the Cessna's path. As soon as the aircraft was steady again, Green called Berlin Military Control, asking them to keep everyone else off the air and to give him a series of courses to steer by radar. The attentions of the two Russian pilots had made it quite impossible to navigate accurately, and if they strayed out of the corridor the jets would have them. By this time they were more than halfway down the 120-mile-long corridor; if they could hold on for a little longer, there might just be a chance.

Seconds later, they knew their luck had run out. The MiG came boring in from astern once more, its cannon twinkling, and the shells were closer than ever before. The Russian pilot, having recovered from his spin, seemed determined to avenge his humiliation.

In the rear of the cockpit, Jim Preston sat tense and white-faced. The two men in the front had their hands full, but Preston could do nothing except sit there helplessly and wait for the killing burst of fire that now seemed almost inevitable. At any second, cannon shells might tear the cockpit and its occupants apart.

The Yak made another close run across the Cessna's path, and a few minutes later the MiG fired another burst past the light aircraft's wingtip. Both Green and Luxton knew that it was all over.

Luxton called Berlin, and told the controller that they had decided to follow the Russians off the corridor. The controller acknowledged the message as Green began a gentle turn to the right, leaving the corridor centre-line and rocking his wings to signal his intentions to the Russians. The two fighters sped away and Green saw them circling beyond the right-hand limit of the corridor, a few miles away.

At that moment, the Berlin Controller's voice sounded over the radio. 'Oscar Kilo, we have you on radar, just leaving the centre-line. Incidentally, you have twenty-seven miles to run to Gatow.'

Green and Luxton looked at one another. Twenty-seven miles: closer than they had believed.

'Okay,' Green yelled over the R/T. 'Give me radar!'

At the same instant, he swung the Cessna's nose back towards Berlin and opened the throttles wide, taking the aircraft in a howling dive towards the cloud layer. The needle of the airspeed indicator went right off the clock and the Cessna shuddered with the strain of the high-powered dive. Luxton glanced back, searching for the Russian fighters, and his heart leapt into his throat. The Russian pilots had detected Green's sudden manoeuvre and were now racing to head off the Cessna, the delta-winged MiG-21 – the faster of the two – closing the distance with terrifying speed. It opened fire just as the Cessna plunged into the shelter of the cloud.

All the while, Berlin Control was passing radar courses for Green to steer. He concentrated on following them while the Cessna's other two occupants held their breath. Around them, the clouds turned red with the glare of the MiG's exploding cannon-shells. This time, the Russian meant business; he was out to kill them. They thanked their lucky stars that it wasn't the Yak-25, with its radar-directed fire control system, which had followed them down into the murk.

They continued their descent, still following Berlin's radar steers, and dropped out of the overcast soon afterwards. Dead ahead of them was the most beautiful sight they had ever seen – Gatow airfield, ablaze with light under the lowering greyness of the clouds. As Green made an effortless landing, Luxton glanced at his watch, and realized with a shock that their engagement with the Soviet fighters had lasted close on forty minutes.

Some time later, they were taken in a staff car to the HQ British Forces, Berlin, where they were interrogated. The Military Commander appeared to be satisfied that their clearances had been in order, and the matter was passed to the British Embassy in Bonn.

Green and his colleagues, however, soon discovered that their problems were only just beginning, for the Embassy was unable to obtain the necessary clearance for them to fly the Cessna out of Berlin. A couple of days later, after Green's show, they caught a scheduled BEA Viscount back to London. Green at once made further inquiries, only to be told that, despite repeated requests, the Russians had still not given permission for the return flight. However, an official said, if they were prepared to take a big chance and fly the Cessna out at their own risk, then under the circumstances the British Embassy would turn a blind eye.

Green and Luxton decided that the gamble was worth taking, and caught the next Viscount back to Berlin. The following morning, at dawn, they took off from Gatow under strict radio silence and set out towards Hanover along the centre air corridor, the shortest of the three, flying at low level to minimize the risk of detection by Soviet radar. Also, the two pilots reasoned that if they were intercepted, their low altitude would give hostile fighters little room for manoeuvre.

They need not have worried; no other aircraft was sighted and they made the sixty-mile dash in twenty minutes, hedge-hopping all the way. Safely out of the corridor, they climbed and contacted Hanover Control, who cleared them to London.

Later, after further enquiries, Hughie Green established that the appropriate clearance for his initial flight to Berlin had never been obtained from the Soviet authorities. He charged the then Soviet leader, Nikita Khrushchev, with an 'outrageous attack on a civil aircraft' and the Ministry of Aviation with 'gross negligence' in giving him clearance to fly through the Berlin Corridor without having informed the Russians. The Russians denied the charge; the Ministry of Aviation paid him £303 damages and a further £100 to charity at Green's request.

Some time after the incident, Green sent a message via the Soviet Embassy to the Red Air Force pilots who had come so close to killing him, inviting them to appear on his television show.

They declined.

11 Combat Over Sinai

At 0715 Cairo time on the morning of 5 June 1967 a twin-engined Ilyushin 14 droned over the Suez Canal at 10,000 feet, heading eastwards into the Sinai Peninsula. The aircraft had been fitted out as an airborne command post; this morning, in addition to its normal crew, it carried three high-ranking officers – General Mohammed Sidki, the commander-in-chief of the Egyptian Air Force, General Amer, the Egyptian Chief of Staff, and a Soviet Air Force brigadier-general who was attached to the EAF as a liaison officer.

Sidki had been a worried man for the past two days. He was convinced that the Israelis, under the threat of invasion from their hostile Arab neighbours, were planning a pre-emptive strike; what he did not know was when it would take place. It was logical to assume, however, that such a strike would come at first light, and the Soviet adviser thought so too. Accordingly, Sidki had ordered two squadrons of MiG-17s and MiG-21s to patrol Israel's border with Sinai for the hour following sunrise at 0400; after that, from 0500 until 0700, Egyptian fighters had been flying half-hourly 'cab rank' patrols along the length of the Suez Canal. At 0705, a couple of minutes after the last patrol became airborne, Sidki and Amer had also taken off in their Il-14 to make an assessment of the situation; in the aircraft's fuselage four electronics operators sat huddled over their equipment, tuned in to the Israeli frequencies and listening for any tell-tale radio chatter that might indicate unusual air activity.

There was nothing; the Israeli military frequencies were silent.

The Il-14 droned on over Sinai, covering the territory in a broad circle while the officers on board surveyed the Egyptian positions spread out beneath them. The crew of the Ilyushin were unaware that they were being continuously tracked by Israeli radar, or that the aircraft's progress was causing a good deal of anxiety among the officers assembled in the main Israeli operations room; if the Il-14 turned north towards Gaza and lingered in the vicinity of Israel's border, its occupants would almost certainly detect the armada of attack aircraft that would soon be skimming low over the Peninsula towards their objectives in the Canal Zone. An audible sigh of relief went up when the radar plot indicated that the Ilyushin had turned south and was heading for the Gulf of Akaba; for the moment, the danger was over.

At 0745, the sky over Hatzor, Ekron, Lod and Ramat David – the airfield complex clustered like a shield round the heart of Israel – trembled with the thunder of jet engines as the first wave of Israeli attack aircraft took off, staying low down and hugging the shadow of the Judaean Hills. On the other side of those hills lay danger. Beyond the morning mist that still lay over the valley of the Jordan, at Ajlun on the slopes of the 4,000-foot Jebel Umed Daraj, the scanner of an ultra-modern Jordanian Marconi 547 surveillance radar conducted a never-ending search of the sky over Israel. Only by keeping down behind the hills, where the radar's probing beams could not penetrate, could the Israeli aircraft hope to escape detection.

Still holding down below the line of the horizon, the first wave of aircraft – French-built Dassault Mirages – sped low over the sweeping curve of the Israeli coast just south of Yafo. There were twenty-four of them in battle formation, comprising six flights of four aircraft.

The Mirages swept out over the Mediterranean at a steady 500 knots, 150 feet above the waves, rocking slightly as they skimmed through patches of turbulence. They were heavily laden with fuel; in addition to the 730 gallons carried in its internal tanks, each Mirage carried two auxiliary fuel pods slung beneath its wings.

Nestling beside these pods, one under each wing, was the war-load: a slim, eight-foot bomb of a type never before used under operational conditions. The weapon, originally projected by Engins Matra of France and subsequently developed in Israel, was designed to be dropped from a low-level strike aircraft flying at between 300 and 500 knots, at a height of 300 feet above ground level. The bomb was fitted with a battery of four small retro-rockets, set to fire automatically exactly three-tenths of a second after release, slowing the weapon and causing it to nose down towards its objective – the concrete surface of a runway – at an angle of eighty degrees. Another six-tenths of a second and a small drogue parachute would deploy, stabilizing the bomb in its descent. Then, just under two seconds after launch, would come the last stage in the automatic sequence of events: the firing of four solid-fuel booster rockets, fitted in the tail section of the device. These would burn away the drogue parachute and accelerate the bomb to a speed of over 500 feet per second. Under the drive of the rockets, the bomb's 365-pound high explosive warhead would break through the runway surface and explode, causing a shallow crater and distortion of the concrete over a radius of several yards.

Just a couple of these weapons, dropped on a runway intersection, would be sufficient to prevent the runways being used by jet combat aircraft – for several hours at least. The main advantage of the weapon, which weighed just over 1,000 pounds, over more conventional bombs was that it could be delivered with great accuracy even by a pilot of average skill, thanks to an advanced sighting system.

But the pilots who were carrying this bomb into action on this brilliant morning were more than average. They were drawn from the ranks of the most experienced aircrews in an air force which boasted one of the highest standards of training and efficiency of any in the world. In the Mirage III CJ, too, they possessed one of the world's finest combat aircraft: a machine capable of doubling as an interceptor, strike or reconnaissance aircraft, depending on the role operational necessity demanded of it.

The Mirages were the spearhead of the 150-strong air strike

force which the Israelis had launched against Egyptian targets on this fateful June morning. The remainder of the force consisted of Dassault Ouragans, Mystères, Super Mystères and twin-engined Sud-Aviation Vautour jets, all targeted to hit eleven key Egyptian airfields – seven in Egypt itself and four in Sinai. The latter were El Arish, Bir Gifgafa, Bir Thamada and Jebel Libni; the Egyptian mainland bases were Abu Sueir, Kabrit, Inchas, Cairo West, El Mansura, Beni-Sueif and Fayid.

The attack force followed three separate routes. The strongest element flew in a broad curve, heading south and then southeast across the Nile Delta to strike at the Egyptian bases in the Canal Zone and deeper inland; a second element, after flying out across the sea, turned inland to hit three of the Sinai bases; while the third element flew south at low level to attack El Arish. Every pilot had been given a detailed briefing on the exact position of enemy radar and anti-aircraft defences and had spent hours studying target maps of his assigned airfield, so that no time would be wasted in searching for the dispersals that sheltered the MiG-21 fighters and Tu-16 jet bombers that formed the core of the Egyptian Air Force's offensive and defensive strength.

At 0810 Cairo time, the Ilyushin 14 carrying General Mohammed Sidki turned north-westwards, its reconnaissance flight over, and headed for its base at Kabrit. The pilot called up Kabrit tower and informed the controller of his ETA. The controller acknowledged; there was no traffic and everything was normal. Suddenly, at 0815, a confused babble of voices burst over the R/T. The pilot called up Kabrit again; there was no reply. The frequencies were jammed by incoherent chatter in which the words 'we are being attacked' were repeated over and over again.

The minutes ticked by. Sidki, in an agony of frustration, knew that his worst fears had materialized – but he still had no idea of the true situation. Then, with twenty-five miles still to go before the Ilyushin reached the Suez Canal, the crew saw the first mushrooms of smoke.

The whole Canal zone seemed to be on fire. The Egyptian airfields were shattered, littered with the wreckage of combat aircraft. The Il-14 pilot flew the length of the canal, but could find nowhere to land. On Sidki's orders, he turned eastwards again and headed for the Sinai airfield of Bir Gifgafa. That, too, was in ruins; so were its neighbours, their runways pock-marked with bomb craters. There was nothing for it but to fly back across the canal in the hope of finding a serviceable airstrip. Finally, the Ilyushin was cleared to land at Cairo International airport at 1015, two hours after the first air strikes took place. Desperately, Sidki tried to salvage something from the chaos, to organize a scratch combat force from the remnants of his squadrons, but as more situation reports reached him, he realized that it was hopeless. There was nothing left; the Egyptian Air Force had been reduced to scrap metal in the space of two hours. Sidki's carefully-laid operational plans had been torn to shreds by rockets, bombs and cannon-shells; the Israeli Air Force was mistress of the sky.

The first massive air strike had done its work well – far better, in fact, than even General Mordecai Hod, the Israeli Air Force C-in-C, had dared to hope. As planned, the first airfield to be hit was Cairo West, where the Mirage pilots found several Tupolev T-16 jet bombers of the 65th Air Brigade parked in their blast-proof revetments. After neutralizing the runways on their first pass, the Israeli pilots turned their attention to the bombers, destroying sixteen with cannon fire in the space of five minutes.

There were more Tu-16s at Beni Sueif, on the Nile to the south of Cairo. This airfield was hit first of all by Vautours, closely followed by Mirages. Arriving over the enemy base, the Mirages found very little left; tall columns of smoke rose from blazing aircraft everywhere, testifying to the accuracy of the Vautours. However, the Mirages shot up four MiG-21s which had escaped the first attack, and destroyed the last four surviving Tu-16s, which were taxi-ing out for take-off.

The fast, swept-wing Tu-16, thirty of which had been supplied to Egypt by the Soviet Union, had been a source of anxiety to the Israelis ever since the 65th Air Brigade had received the type. It was able to carry up to 20,000 pounds of bombs, and its range of 3,000 miles meant that it could strike at targets in Israel from any Arab base. With all thirty Tu-16s now out of action, the only bombers the Egyptians had left were thirty-five elderly twin-jet Ilyushin Il-28s, equipping three squadrons of the 61st Air Brigade. Although far less formidable than the Tu-16, they nevertheless posed a threat of considerable proportions, so General Hod gave priority to their destruction.

The Il-28s were based on two airfields, Luxor and Ras Banas, from where they had taken part in the Egyptian Air Force's offensive against Yemeni Royalists during the preceding months. Because of the Egyptian High Command's belief that the bases were far enough south to be safe from Israeli air attack, no attempt had been made to disperse the bombers.

It therefore came as a severe shock when, at 0830, four Vautours suddenly appeared at low level over Luxor and made several passes over the line of parked Il-28s, causing considerable havoc with their 30-millimetre cannon. During the final pass one Vautour was hit by anti-aircraft fire and crashed on top of a section of four MiG-17 fighters, which erupted in an enormous mushroom of burning fuel.

Meanwhile, four more Vautours, led by Lieutenant-Colonel Dani, had taken off from an airstrip in the Negev Desert and set out on the 500-mile flight to Ras Banas. Each aircraft carried two 500-pound bombs and maximum fuel. Because of the distance involved, there could be no question of making the trip at low level; the aircraft climbed steeply to 24,000 feet and then levelled off, the pilots shutting down one engine to obtain the maximum economical cruise. The Vautours headed due south, crossing the Gulf of Akaba and flying along the Red Sea after skimming the fringes of Saudi Arabian territory. Then, nearly an hour and a half after take-off, the pilots relit their number two engines and made a fast descent towards Ras Banas. The Egyptian defences were taken by surprise and the Vautours hurtled across the airfield, dropping their bombs on the runways and then turning to rake the Il-28s with their cannon. All the Vautours escaped unharmed, leaving the wrecks of sixteen bombers behind them.

By 0830 the first wave of Israeli jets had completed their strikes on Egyptian targets west of the Suez Canal and were on their way home to refuel and re-arm for a second mission. In the meantime, other IAF fighter-bombers had struck hard at the four enemy bases in Sinai. At Jebel Libni, for example, two Egyptian pilots of the 25th Fighter Squadron were sitting in the cockpits of their MiG-17s on readiness, with their battery trollies plugged in and all ready to go, when four Israeli Mystères swept over the airfield and dropped their rocket-powered bombs on the runway intersection. While the dust and smoke of the explosions still hung in the air one pair of Mystères racked round in a tight turn, streaked back towards the two MiGs and opened fire with their 30-millimetre cannon. The MiG pilots died in their cockpits and the aircraft crumpled into the dust, blazing fiercely.

The other two Mystères, meanwhile, had dived down to strafe the thirteen MiG-17s and MiG-19s parked near the airfield buildings. Several were knocked out during the fighters' first pass, and the destruction was completed when the four Mystères joined forces and made two more low-level runs. Several dummy MiGs were completely ignored; apart from the fact that IAF Intelligence had been aware of them, they were parked at the side of the runway and in other unlikely places where no genuine aircraft would have been deployed.

Attacking Jebel Libni had called for a high degree of precision, for the Israeli pilots had been briefed to leave 3,500 feet of the airfield's 7,000-foot runway undamaged so that it could be used by IAF transport aircraft at a later stage. To forestall any Egyptian attempt to repair the runways, three flights of Mystères and Ouragans hit the airfield again at dusk and showered it with small delayed-action bombs, set to detonate throughout the night.

El Arish, too, was required for use by the IAF Air Transport Command, and the Israelis took a calculated risk in leaving its runways completely intact. However, the six MiG-17s that were based there were knocked out by rocket-firing Super Mystères, and the Israelis flew continual combat patrols over the airfield until their ground forces captured it later.

Despite the element of surprise, Israeli aircraft attacking the other two Sinai bases, Bir Gifgafa and Bir Thamada, found themselves opposed by Egyptian fighters. At Bir Gifgafa, four Vautours led by Captain Aaron were intercepted by four MiG-21s; two Vautours took them on while the other pair raced across the airfield and dropped their bombs. Three of the MiGs immediately vanished behind the dense cloud of smoke and dust kicked up by the bomb-bursts; the fourth stayed to fight, turning in towards no. 4 Vautour and launching an air-to-air missile. The Israeli pilot took violent evasive action at very low level and the weapon missed its target. Vautour no. 1 then got on the MiG's tail and opened fire, but its cannon shells also went wide of the mark and the Egyptian pilot turned away, heading towards the Suez Canal at high speed. The Vautours resumed their attack on the airfield, diving through the smoke to strafe some Il-28 bombers and Il-14 transports.

Bir Thamada was attacked by four Ouragans, with four Mirages flying top cover. A MiG-21 was in the act of taking off as the Ouragans dived down to make their first strafing run in line astern and the leader broke away, firing a long burst at it; the MiG hit the ground and skidded along on its belly, shedding fragments. The Ouragans knocked out the runways and destroyed four Il-14s with cannon fire, then curved round to attack a trio of helicopters on the far side of the field. One of them, a giant Mil Mi-6, had just got airborne and was hanging in mid-air at the point of transition from hovering to forward flight when a burst of cannon shells from the leading Ouragan scythed off its main rotor. The mighty fuselage dropped to the ground like a stone and burst into flames. The other two helicopters were destroyed on the ground. Several more Egyptian transports, including a big Antonov An-12, were knocked out during a strike by Mystères on Bir Thamada later that morning.

At 1000 hours the second series of air strikes on the Egyptian airfields across the Suez Canal got under way. The first devastating strike wave had hit its targets and escaped relatively unscathed, but now the Egyptian anti-aircraft defences were fully alerted and subsequent strikes began to suffer losses as they ran into heavy defensive fire and some air opposition. At about

1010, a whirling dogfight developed over Abu Sueir between sixteen Mirages and twenty MiG-21s, which had flown hurriedly north from Hurghada, on the shores of the Red Sea, to cover the south-eastern approaches to the Canal zone. The Egyptian pilots hurled themselves on the Mirages, but they were hopelessly out-classed; four of the MiGs were shot down in a matter of minutes, and the rest – probably critically low on fuel – broke off the engagement and headed west, looking for somewhere to land. A few managed to get down safely, but most smashed themselves to pieces while attempting to land on shattered runways or were destroyed when the pilots ejected after their aircraft ran out of fuel.

Half an hour later, Mirages made an air strike on Hurghada to neutralize the remaining MiG-21s that were known to be based there. A few MiGs got into the air to intercept the attack-ers, but were driven off. One of them fired an air-to-air missile at one of the Israeli aircraft; it missed its target, but its heat-seeking guidance system locked on to another MiG-21 and destroyed it. Another Mirage pilot, flying low to the south of the Nile Delta towards his assigned target, together with three other Mirages, flew into an intense anti-aircraft barrage; they got clear of it without harm, and then :

> We went into a shallow dive to attack Cairo West, levelling out at 200 feet and taking evasive action to avoid more anti-aircraft fire. Suddenly, I saw a SAM-2 ground-to-air missile approaching me, only about 300 feet away; I turned sharply and it passed underneath my Mirage and exploded on the enemy airfield. A second rocket appeared above me and curved towards my aircraft, approaching at an angle of about thirty degrees to the nose. The thing looked like a telephone pole, with flames streaming out of the back. I turned hard right and it passed over my nose. I suppose I was lucky, but I think the Egyptians must have been firing the SAMs visually, without using their radar guidance system.

By 1100, all the designated Egyptian airfields except one had been attacked. The exception was Fayid, which had escaped the first strike because it was shrouded by fog that had drifted over it from the nearby Bitter Lake. It was attacked by Ouragans at 1015; they knocked out several MiG-19s, MiG-21s and two Sukhoi Su-7 fighter-bombers, the latest in the line of combat aircraft supplied to Egypt by the Soviet Union.

Elsewhere, Israeli pilots returning with the second and third strike waves found a shortage of targets. One Super Mystère pilot, leading a flight of four aircraft to Kabrit just before 1100, reported:

> Every aircraft on the base had already been destroyed, so we attacked the hangars and fuel dump. On the way back we spotted a train halfway between Cairo and the Canal and radioed control for permission to attack it, but this was refused on the grounds that it was probably not a military target. Instead, we were ordered across the Canal to hit targets in Sinai.

Meanwhile, at 1045, the Royal Jordanian Air Force had entered the battle when four Hawker Hunter fighter-bombers from Mafraq strafed the Israeli forward airstrip of Kefar Sirkin, just across the border, knocking out two light aircraft and a few vehicles. The Hunters returned to their base to find it under attack by IAF Mirages, which the Jordanian pilots promptly engaged. One Hunter was shot down almost at once, the pilot ejecting; the others managed to land safely when shortage of fuel brought an end to the combat, although they were all destroyed on the ground in later attacks. Two Hunters were destroyed while awaiting permission to take off at the end of Mafraq's runway, one of the pilots being killed by cannon shells as he tried to get out of his aircraft. He was the only Jordanian pilot to die during the June War, although others were injured; these included the pilot who ejected, breaking his back.

By noon, Israeli strike aircraft had practically wiped out Jordan's small air force, and the IAF now turned its attention to Syria and Iraq. At about 1315, a lone Iraqi Tu-16 came in low over the Plain of Sharon and bombed the Israeli town of Netanya, astride the main Haifa-Tel Aviv railway line; it was shot down by 40-millimetre anti-aircraft batteries. This was the only foray made into Israel by the Iraqi Air Force; an hour later, Israeli Mirages and Mystères hit Habbaniyah and the airstrip designated 'Hotel Three', destroying nine MiG-21s, five Hunters and two Il-14 transports. The Iraqis possessed a large number of modern Soviet combat aircraft and the damage suffered in this attack was relatively light, but – possibly because of Soviet pressure – their air force took no further part in the conflict and the Israelis left it alone.

The main reason why Iraq was spared a crushing air strike on 5 June – apart from the range involved and the lack of availability of strike aircraft – was that the IAF, having destroyed the greater part of the EAF and almost the whole of the RJAF, was now preoccupied with Syria. The Syrian air bases at Seikel, Dumeyr, Damascus, Marj Rhiyal and Tango Four were heavily attacked by Mirages, Mystères and Super Mystères, which destroyed thirty-two MiG-21s, twenty-three MiG-17s and -15s, two Il-28s and three Mi-4 helicopters. Anti-aircraft fire was heavy and several Israeli aircraft were shot down; the total included two Mystères, destroyed over Damascus. Another Mystère was jumped by a flight of MiG-17s, which shot it down as it was attacking targets on the ground; the MiGs were themselves shot down by Mirages a few minutes later. The Syrians proved to be aggressive pilots, but time after time the superior tactics and training of the Israelis paid off, even when confronted by formidable odds. During one attack on Seikal, two Super Mystères – flown by Lieutenants Yermi and Yallo – were attacked by four MiG-21s, aircraft which outclassed the French-built types in every respect except, perhaps, manoeuvrability. Yallo, a 32-year-old veteran, got in a deflection shot at one of the MiGs and saw it explode, but failed to see another MiG coming down fast on his tail. He was saved by Yermi, who curved in to the attack, and fired a long burst; his cannon shells struck home and the Syrian fighter began to lose height, trailing smoke. The pilot ejected before the MiG hit the ground.

While the fast Israeli jets were occupied in neutralizing the enemy air forces, the Israeli ground offensive had been supported almost entirely by squadrons of Fouga Magisters, little training aircraft which now assumed the ground-attack role with devastating effect, their wings laden with 68- and 80-millimetre rockets. The Magister pilots, many of them reservists, were low-level specialists in the truest sense, and just how low they flew was proclaimed by a large warning notice on the wall of one of their briefing rooms: 'When operating over Jordanian territory, watch out for telephone wires!'

In the words of one Magister pilot, a reserve lieutenant who had been in New York at the beginning of June and who had returned to Israel just in time for the outbreak of hostilities:

'We got right down on the deck, kicking up the dust and flying at about the same height as the targets we were attacking. On several occasions, I saw the heads of the enemy tank commanders silhouetted above the turrets. We were so low they couldn't bring their guns to bear on us. We usually managed to knock them out on the first pass; our rockets were in fairly short supply so we didn't want to waste them. We used our machine-guns against soft-skinned targets.'

On the Jordanian front alone, the Magisters knocked out fifty tanks and over seventy other vehicles on 5 and 6 June. The shortage of air-to-ground rockets was alleviated on the morning of the sixth, when the Israelis captured El Arish airfield; they found hundreds of 80-millimetre rockets, all of them manufactured by the Swiss firm of Oerlikon and identical with those used by the IAF. They kept the Magister squadrons supplied until the end of the fighting.

No air strikes were carried out against enemy airfields on Tuesday, 6 June; instead, the Israeli fighter squadrons flew ground-attack missions or top cover over the battlefield, and they were frequently challenged by hostile jets. One of the first combats of the day came at 0600, when two Sukhoi Su-7 fighter-bombers raced up to attack Israeli armour which was refuelling on the outskirts of El Arish. Before they reached their target, however, the Egyptians were intercepted by a pair of Mirages, which shot both of them down into the desert.

The Su-7s put in several appearances on the sixth, and if the

Egyptians had had more of these fast, potent jets they might have constituted a serious threat. But only fifteen of them were in Egypt at the beginning of June, equipping a reserve squadron of the 12th Air Division, and their pilots had orders to avoid combat whenever possible. Nevertheless, by nightfall on the sixth the Israeli fighter pilots had claimed the destruction of twelve of them, one after a spectacular chase by a Mirage across Sinai at Mach 1.1. The Israeli pilot opened fire at two hundred yards and saw the Su-7's tail unit disintegrate, followed by a bright surge of yellow flame. The Sukhoi reared up sharply, then dropped like a stone into the desert and exploded.

By nightfall on 6 June, with Israeli forces breaking through enemy resistance everywhere in Sinai, the Egyptian Air Force had lost 319 aircraft and helicopters, all but a handful of which had been destroyed on the ground. The total included all thirty Tu-16s of the Strategic Bombing Wing; twenty-seven Il-28s, most of which were destroyed in the Vautour strikes on Luxor and Ras Banas in the south: the twelve Su-7s; ninety-five MiG-21s; twenty-five MiG-19s; eighty-five MiG-15s and MiG-17s; twenty-four Ilyushin 14 and eight Antonov An-12 transports; eight Mi-6, four Mi-1 and one Mi-4 helicopters. On the other fronts, the Syrians had lost two Il-28s, thirty-two MiG-21s, twenty-three MiG-15s and MiG-17s and three helicopters, while Iraq had lost one Tu-16, nine MiG-21s, five Hunters and five Il-14s. The unfortunate RJAF had been virtually wiped out, losing twenty-one Hunters, five transport aircraft and three helicopters. The last Arab air casualty was a Lebanese Hunter, which infiltrated Israeli air space late on Tuesday and was promptly shot down by a Mirage patrol.

On the other side, IAF losses at the end of the second day of fighting stood at twenty-six aircraft: seven Mystère IVAs, five Ouragans, four Super Mystères, two Mirages, seven Magisters and one Vautour. None of the Israeli aircraft had been destroyed in actual air combat, although three Mystères had been 'bounced' by MiGs during strafing attacks on enemy airfields. Five of the shot-down Israeli pilots baled out over friendly territory or were picked up by rescue helicopters; of the remaining twenty-one, eight were killed, ten were taken prisoner and three were reported missing.

On the morning of 7 June, with complete air superiority now in their grasp, the Israelis turned the full fury of their air onslaught against the Egyptian forces in Sinai, now in full retreat towards two positions where they might hope to block the Israeli advance : Bir Gifgafa and Mitla. In the late afternoon, a neck-and-neck race for the Mitla Pass developed between the leading Egyptian columns and an Israeli armoured battalion. The Israelis got there first and set up a roadblock, but with only nine tanks left they were unable to stem the enemy flood. The leading Egyptian tanks broke through the pass and charged on towards the Suez Canal and safety. Then the Israeli jets arrived overhead. One Ouragan pilot reported :

> We went straight for the western end of the pass and found an echelon of eight Egyptian tanks just emerging from it. We knocked all of them out with rocket fire, and as we turned for home we saw a disorganized mass of armour and trucks beginning to pile up in the bottleneck. We called Operations and told them to order the strike aircraft following us to get a move on, for we had presented them with a once-in-a-lifetime target.

The slaughter went on hour after hour, as flights of Israeli fighter-bombers hammered the column of 1,500 Egyptian tanks and vehicles trapped at Mitla. Meanwhile, another armoured division under General Israel Tal had been driving rapidly towards Ismailia, with Bir Gifgafa as its primary objective. At about 1530 on Wednesday, the leading units became involved in a fierce skirmish with enemy tanks near Bir Gifgafa airfield, and a few minutes later two flights of MiG-17s whistled up and made several high-speed strafing runs over the Israeli column. The enemy jets were engaged by Mystères, but on this occasion the Israelis got the worst of the encounter; one Mystère was shot down and the MiGs got away. As a demonstration of Egyptian air power it was hardly impressive, but it showed that the EAF – although no longer in any position to offer a challenge to Israeli air superiority – was still capable of hitting back. The fighter-bombers that were sent into action now were mostly aircraft that had been dispersed on airfields deep inside Egypt at the time of the Israeli air strike on 5 June, but a few were Algerian machines with their national markings painted out. They had been sent to Egypt following a desperate plea from President Nasser for aircraft to cover the retreat of the Egyptian forces from Sinai; although the majority were flown by Egyptians, Algerian pilots also took part in the attacks on several occasions. More MiGs attacked the Israeli column that was advancing along the Ismailia axis before nightfall, but this time the Mirages were waiting for them and three of the enemy aircraft were destroyed.

Thursday, the last day of the Sinai campaign, was marked by some of the most savage fighting in the Six-Day War as the Egyptians hurled their last reserves across the Canal in a desperate attempt to stem the Israeli advance for long enough to allow their shattered armies to escape. The Egyptian tank crews fought with suicidal courage; of the 950 tanks committed to the fighting in Sinai, only about a hundred fell intact into Israeli hands. The remainder fought on until they were destroyed by Israeli armour and anti-tank guns or knocked out by the air strikes. The EAF went on hitting the advancing Israeli columns with sporadic hit-and-run attacks; these were pressed home with fierce determination, and some of them inflicted considerable damage. But the courage of the Egyptian pilots was not enough; the prowling Mirages and Mystères were everywhere, and the fighter-bombers suffered appalling losses.

Nevertheless, the IAF did not have everything its own way during the closing stages of the campaign. Shortly before dusk on Thursday, following the capture of Kantara by Israeli forces, the IAF was called in to attack several formations of Egyptian tanks that were fighting back fiercely on the Ismailia axis. The jets inflicted heavy casualties, but they had to attack through a storm of anti-aircraft fire which destroyed three Ouragans and two Mystères. It was the heaviest loss suffered by the IAF during a single attack in the entire Sinai campaign.

By 0300 on Friday, 9 June the fighting in Sinai was over, the Egyptians already having accepted a cease-fire. The Syrians,

131

against whom there had been bitter fighting on the Golan Heights, also accepted a cease-fire several hours later.

The security of the state of Israel had been secured, for the time being at least, with one of the most crushing victories in the history of warfare. It was a victory attributable in the main to the effectiveness of the IAF and it had been bought at a cost of some forty aircraft.

It could never happen again. For when yet another Arab-Israeli war was fought six years later – the Yom Kippur conflict of 1973 – the Egyptians had learned their lesson well, and it was they who enjoyed the element of surprise. Moreover, the Israeli pilots had to contend not only with opponents of a far higher calibre than before, but also with surface-to-air missile screens which meted out fearful punishment to their strike aircraft.

Those six days in the summer of 1967 had marked the close of an era. Never again would an air force administer such a crushing defeat to an enemy, at such minimal cost.

12 Invasion!

It was 2152 hours on 20 August 1968, and the control tower staff at Ruzyne, Prague's international airport, were thankfully coming to the end of a routine but tiring day. Away to the east of the field, landing lights flared brightly in the darkness; an aircraft was on the approach to Runway 25. It was a twin-engined Antonov An-24 turboprop transport belonging to Aeroflot, the Soviet airline, on an unscheduled flight from Moscow. Engines whining shrilly, the Antonov slid over the threshold and touched down smoothly. It came to a stop briefly while the pilot obtained taxi instructions, then turned off the runway and moved towards the concrete apron on the eastern side of the airport buildings. A handful of passengers disembarked and made their way into the terminal.

Meanwhile, in the tower, the duty controllers were stretching their tired limbs. They could afford to relax a little now; the next scheduled aircraft movement was not until 2310, when a Polish Airlines Tupolev 104 jet airliner was due to depart for Teheran. After that, they could go off duty; the next watch was due to take over at 0300, in time for the early morning departure of a Yugoslav Ilyushin 18 for Belgrade.

Despite the outward appearance of normality, the control tower staff at Ruzyne were uneasy. For some time now, their Warsaw Pact neighbours had been showing increasing resentment towards Czechoslovakia's new liberal government, headed by President Svoboda and Premier Dubcek, and the tension had been growing throughout July, as talks aimed at conciliation took place between the Czechs and the Russians.

133

The fact that the Warsaw Pact had been carrying out a series of large-scale military exercises for weeks had done nothing to ease the tension. The manoeuvres had begun on 10 May when two tank armies – one Russian and one Polish, totalling 2,800 tanks and 84,000 men – began operations in southern Poland. Primarily, it was designed to test mobility and the effectiveness of co-operation between large Russian and Polish formations. About 150 combat aircraft, mainly ground-attack types, were also involved in the exercise, together with an unspecified number of large assault helicopters.

This exercise ended on 22 May, but on 10 June the manoeuvres entered a second phase with an exercise on East German territory. Once again, co-operation was the keyword; five Soviet armoured divisions operated in concert with two East German mechanized infantry divisions, and two East German MiG-21 regiments flew top cover for Soviet Yak-28s in a simulated ground-attack exercise.

On 18 June Marshal Ivan Yakubovsky, the Warsaw Pact Commander-in-Chief, set up a temporary headquarters in Prague, from where the third phase of the manoeuvres was to be controlled. This third exercise, known as 'Bohemian Forest', began two days later. Involving some 40,000 men, its purpose – based on the results of the two previous exercises – was to co-ordinate the mobility of the Warsaw Pact land and air forces in Poland, East Germany and Czechoslovakia. The exercise ended on 30 June and all foreign units departed from Czech territory without any fuss, accompanied by sighs of relief from some quarters who believed that the exercise had, in fact, been a brilliant rehearsal for a planned invasion of Czechoslovakia. Significantly, most of the Soviet, Polish and East German units which had taken part in 'Bohemian Forest' remained just on the other side of the Czech border.

Early in July the Soviet Navy held a big exercise in the Baltic, and on the twenty-fourth it was the Soviet Air Force's turn with a massive air exercise known as 'Skyshield'. This covered a triangular area between the Baltic, Moscow and the Black Sea and the whole of the Soviet air defences between Kaliningrad in the north and Odessa in the south remained on full alert for over a month. By 31 July a force of 200 MiG-19 and MiG-21 interceptors, together with about fifty Su-7B ground-attack jets, had been dispersed on airfields in southern Poland. Transport aircraft had flown in full supporting equipment and the Russian combat units showed no sign of leaving in the near future. Three Polish fighter regiments and one ground-attack regiment were also placed on readiness, involving some 160 combat aircraft.

By mid-August, an enormous array of military strength was massed around Czechoslovakia's frontiers. To the north, in Poland, lay Army Group A, with a strength of three Soviet armoured divisions, one Soviet mechanized infantry division, one Soviet airborne division, one Polish mechanized infantry division, one Polish airborne division and a Polish Air Force Division, with MiG-21 fighters and An-12 transports. To the north-west, in East Germany, was Army Group B with three Soviet armoured divisions and one East German mechanized division, with supporting air units, while Army Group C in Hungary, on the southern flank, consisted of Soviet and Hungarian armoured, mechanized infantry and artillery divisions.

At 2203 on 20 August the controllers at Ruzyne were suddenly startled by a call from another Russian aircraft, an Antonov 24, which requested landing clearance. They were puzzled, for they had received no prior warning of the aircraft's arrival. Over the radio, the Russian pilot informed them that he was inbound from Lvov with twenty-five passengers on board. His intention was to land and discharge them, then take off again.

The Antonov touched down and taxied to a stop outside the terminal building. A small group of Russians was waiting for the passengers and greeted them warmly, then they boarded an airport bus which moved off towards Prague. A few minutes later, the Antonov taxied back to the runway and took off again, quickly disappearing into the darkness.

It was then that the tower staff noticed something strange : the first Antonov had vanished from its position on the apron. They spotted it a minute later, parked by the side of the main runway and showing no lights. The senior controller tried to make contact with it over the R/T, meaning to ask the pilot what his intentions were, but there was no answer.

After the fourth attempt the controller gave up. He felt tense and uneasy, and soon afterwards he had even more cause for apprehension when a top-priority signal came clattering over the teleprinter. It was from the Department of the Interior and it read simply : 'QGO. Immediate effect.'

The code-letters QGO meant that all landings and take-offs were to be prohibited at once, until further notice. The controllers went into action quickly, shutting down the airfield and runway lighting and all radio equipment except the R/T. Then they waited, smoking nervously, as the minutes ticked by.

Suddenly, the R/T came to life again. A distorted Russian voice crackled over the air, calling Ruzyne tower. A flight of three Soviet transport aircraft, approximately ten miles northeast of the airfield, was running low on fuel and requested an emergency landing. The senior controller thought quickly; it was his decision alone. It did not take him long to make up his mind. He told the Russian flight leader that the airport was inoperative and that facilities had been closed down for the night, suggesting that the Russians contacted Kbely military air base instead. He waited for an acknowledgement, but none came. The suspense was on again.

Then things began to happen quickly. A huge dark shape slid down out of the eastern sky and rolled along the runway, its landing-lights ablaze. The shocked controllers recognized the bulky contours of a Russian An-12 transport. A giant's roar split the night as its four powerful Ivchenko turboprop engines were slammed into reverse pitch, bringing it to a stop quickly.

The loading-ramp that fitted snugly under the big upswept tail unit came down slowly and a host of shadowy figures came running out of the transport's massive belly, jumping down on to the concrete surface of the runway. There were forty or fifty of them : Russian paratroops, wearing camouflage smocks and in full battle order.

Now, as the huge An-12 thundered off down the runway and climbed away into the night once more, the paratroops fanned out in an extended line and advanced rapidly on the airport buildings. A second aircraft roared in from the darkness, followed quickly by a third. With near-incredible speed, they discharged their cargoes of men and equipment before taking off again to make room for more. The Russian transports had not needed the assistance of Ruzyne control tower for their rapid landing; they already had their own mobile control tower and ground-controlled approach system on the airfield in the shape of the An-24 that was parked by the side of the main runway. The aircraft was crammed with electronic equipment, and it carried a small crew of Soviet Air Force radar specialists. The passengers who had disembarked when the aircraft landed had successfully camouflaged its real purpose.

Within minutes, the Russian paratroops had secured the control tower, the airport switchboard and other strategic points on Ruzyne. The night now reverberated with the roar of engines as a constant stream of Soviet transport aircraft thundered out of the darkness, touching down at the rate of one every fifty seconds. They were mostly An-12s and An-24s with an occasional gigantic An-22 – the biggest transport aircraft in service anywhere in the world at that time. Each transport disgorged its load of men and material; the tanks came first, mostly ASU-57s but with a smaller number of the newer ASU-85s, their long 85-millimetre gun barrels jutting from the squat silhouettes of their turrets. Then came the BTRs, the armoured personnel carriers into which the troops piled with well-rehearsed efficiency. Within minutes, the column was rumbling on its way towards Prague. Bringing up the rear were light and medium artillery, jeeps and radio vehicles.

Thirty minutes after the first of the Soviet transports touched down at Ruzyne, the controllers at Brno airport, 120 miles to the south-east, also picked up a 'distress' signal from what was thought to be a Russian charter aircraft.

Its pilot requested an emergency landing on the grounds that he was short of fuel, and this was approved immediately. The airport's ambulance and fire services were alerted and stood by alongside the runway. A few minutes later the aircraft landed safely, but instead of taxi-ing towards the airport buildings it rolled straight on to the end of the runway, where it stopped. It was another An-24 'flying control tower'. Before the airport authorities had time to take any action, the wheels of the first giant freighter that followed it were hitting the tarmac and seconds later Soviet paratroops were fanning out across the airfield. The major airports of Bratislava and Ostrava were also taken completely by surprise in a similar way.

The Russians also tried the same tactics in an effort to capture the Czech Air Force Headquarters at Kbely, near Prague. It was a vital objective, for if the Czech armed forces chose to resist the invasion, air operations would be directed from here. However, the instant the base commander learned that Soviet and other Warsaw Pact forces were crossing Czechoslovakia's frontiers he took immediate steps to prevent Soviet aircraft landing on the airfield. The precautions were simple enough; he simply ordered his men to park every available vehicle, from fire-tenders to private cars, in long lines right down the middle of all three runways. When the Soviet transports arrived overhead at 0150 hours on 21 August, the pilots found that they were unable to land and had to divert to the already congested airport at Ruzyne. It was not until four hours later that Kbely was finally overrun – by ground forces.

The capture of the Czech airfields by airborne forces had been a masterpiece of planning. By concentrating on civil airports, the planners had successfully avoided any danger of opposition from anti-aircraft defences, and the whole operation had unfolded with astounding speed and efficiency.

By 0200 on 21 August, with the transport aircraft still unloading supplies and reinforcements on the captured airfields and the spearhead of the airborne forces rolling into the darkened, unsuspecting streets of Prague, five thousand tanks were clattering over the frontiers to complete the destruction of an ideal. The rape of Czechoslovakia had begun.

13 The Men Who Rode the Rockets

It was bitterly cold in the tiny, cramped cockpit of the little Bell X-1 rocket research aircraft. It was dark, too, for the X-1 was recessed into the bomb-bay of the B-29 mother ship, toiling laboriously up the sky to 35,000 feet.

Captain Charles Yeager had been in the cockpit for forty-five minutes now, his knees pulled up to his chin and his feet level with the seat in a vain, huddled attempt to keep warm. His back was against the X-1's liquid oxygen tank, which had a temperature of 140° C below zero, and despite his heated pressure suit the icy cold was slowly eating into his body.

'Chuck' Yeager, aged twenty-four, was one of the United States Air Force's leading test pilots, a member of the small and highly skilled band of men whose task it was to put new combat aircraft through their paces before they were cleared for operational service. Normally based at the USAF Test Flight Division, Wright Field, Dayton, Ohio, Yeager had been transferred to Muroc in California to fly the rocket-propelled X-1, which had been designed by the Bell Aircraft Company for research in the region of the sound barrier.

At the end of World War II, pushing aircraft to the speed of sound and beyond had been seen as the next major breakthrough in jet aircraft design, but the problems had appeared enormous. German designers had researched the effects of supersonic flight with the aid of high-speed wind tunnels, and aircraft such as the jet-propelled Messerschmitt 262 and rocket-powered Me 163 had flown at high subsonic speeds, but the handful of pilots who had pushed their aircraft to the edge of the speed of sound had usually not lived to tell the tale, their machines shaken apart by severe compressibility. Mach 1, as the speed of sound was designated under the scale first devised by the Austrian Professor Ernst Mach in 1887, had become a magic number, and the first man to pass it and survive was assured of a place in aviation history.

In layman's terms, Mach I is equal to a speed of 760.98 mph at sea level at a temperature of 15°C, falling to a constant 659.78 mph above 36,098 feet. To probe into these speed realms, joint design studies were begun soon after the war's end by Bell, the National Advisory Committee for Aeronautics and the USAF; the result was the X-1, a sleek, bullet-shaped aircraft with straight, ultra-thin wings and conventional tail surfaces. It was powered by a Reaction Motors bi-fuel rocket motor capable of developing a maximum static thrust of 6,000 pounds for two and a half minutes, for in the mid 1940s no jet engine had yet been developed that was capable of boosting an aircraft to much more than 600 mph.

In the autumn of 1946 the X-1 made its first flight, being carried to altitude under a modified B-29 bomber and then released to glide to earth. The first flight under its own power was made over the Muroc Flight Test Base on 9 December that year. By the time Yeager joined the test programme in the summer of 1947 the X-1 had made several flights, the speed being pushed up steadily to beyond the 600 mph mark, and much information had been assembled on the aircraft's handling characteristics.

Now, on 14 October 1947, Yeager already had eight flights in the X-1 to his credit, and the ninth promised to be the most important of all. On this bright, warm California morning, if all went well, he would become the first man in history to fly faster than sound.

He had risen at 0600, and his wife, Glennis, had prepared a particularly rich breakfast, with lots of eggs, ham and coffee. He would be grateful for it later, in the cold reaches of the stratosphere. Afterwards, he had set off on his usual thirty-mile motorcycle ride to Muroc, which was later to be renamed Edwards Air Force Base. During the journey his thoughts were occupied with many things; not only with the coming flight, but also with memories of the men who had already died in attempting what he himself hoped to achieve today. Only two months earlier, an Englishman, Geoffrey de Havilland, had been killed when his little swept-wing DH 108 Swallow jet broke apart in a high-speed dive.

Yeager arrived at Muroc to find the ground crew already hard at work preparing the X-1 and the B-29 mother ship for the flight. On the X-1's nose, the name *Glamorous Glennis* stood out boldly in red, outlined in blue. That had been the idea of Jack Roussel, Yeager's Crew Chief.

After a lengthy briefing, together with the six-man crew of the B-29 and other personnel who were to be involved in the mission, Yeager put on his pressure suit, parachute, helmet, electrically heated gloves and insulated boots and joined the B-29 crew on board the mother ship. When it reached 7,000 feet, he clambered into the cockpit of the X-1 and settled down as best he could to wait for the B-29 to reach the launch altitude. During the last few thousand feet he busied himself in checking the rows of vital dials and switches in readiness for the drop, looking up from time to time to watch oxygen-masked crew members topping up the X-1's liquid oxygen tank. This had been filled to capacity before take-off, but Lox is an unnatural substance, a gas compressed into a liquid state. If it is not kept under constant pressure the liquid reverts to a gas rapidly and explosively. Since the Lox tended to evaporate quickly during the long climb to height, topping up the tank was a constant task. Nor was liquid oxygen the only worry. Behind the Lox tank was a second highly volatile fuel, alcohol. A controlled combination of the two would provide the power that would thrust the X-1 to its maximum speed, but any accidental contact between the fuels during the topping-up procedure would result in a blinding explosion that would totally destroy both aircraft and their occupants. Yeager said later:

Waiting to be dropped is perhaps the biggest scare. At 1050 the B-29 pilot asked me if I was ready over the radio and I replied 'Yes'. 'Okay,' he said, and then counted. 'Thirty seconds more . . . twenty seconds . . . ten seconds . . . nine . . . eight . . . seven . . . six . . . five . . . four . . . three . . . two . . . one . . . drop!'

I dropped. It felt as though I was on top of a roller coaster. All around me it was bright. It was a few seconds before I could see again. It was like being under tremendous glaring lights.

As soon as I dropped, I began pulling back the control stick to stop the fall. Still falling, I turned on the rocket motor — three of its four tubes. Immediately the plane began climbing. It zoomed up to 42,000 feet in less than a minute. I levelled off and fired the fourth tube. 'I am firing number four now,' I shouted into the mike, 'I am beginning to run.' The plane pulled off at full power. Some of the most thrilling moments in my flying career had come.

The plane accelerated with frightening convulsions. It shook and buffeted terribly for about thirty seconds until I got it up to about Mach 1. Then the buffeting left off, but the plane still shook strongly. It was very hard to control, and I had to fly carefully to prevent it turning over. I was too busy to speak into the microphone. Security regulations forbade me, anyway, to tell the others how fast I was going and that men now could fly at supersonic speed.

The Mach needle went higher. I took the speed up to Mach 1.05 and kept it there for about fifteen or twenty seconds. Then I turned off the rocket motor. Not more than two and a half minutes had passed since I had started it. As the plane slowed down the buffeting began again. I jettisoned the remaining fuel overboard; at take-off I had had 600 gallons. Gliding down for about ten minutes, I talked to the people on the ground. I said that it was a very successful flight. I think they understood what I meant. Then we joked about the weather.

All the time two chase planes, F-80 jets, had tried to follow me, but I could not find them any more. *Glamorous Glennis* had left them far behind. I told the ground crew where I would land and to have the fire trucks there. Landing was easy. The plane stopped rolling, and I turned off the radio and switches. The ground crew helped me remove the doors as I got out. I was tired and exhausted and frozen; it felt good to be back on the warm ground of Lake Muroc. There was no ceremony or big congratulating. For all of us this was work, hard work. And security was involved.

Charles E. Yeager went on to make fifty-three more flights in the X-1, most of them at supersonic speed. On 5 January 1949 he took the aircraft off the ground for the first time under its own power and climbed to 23,000 feet in one minute forty seconds, exceeding the speed of sound on the climb, and in February 1948 he pushed the rocket plane past the 1,000 mph mark.

Flight at twice the speed of sound now seemed an attainable goal, and in 1950 the Bell X-1 was joined at Muroc by another rocket research aircraft, the Douglas Skyrocket. This sleek, swept-wing aircraft was originally powered by both turbojet and rocket motors, enabling a normal take-off to be made from the ground. Later, the turbojet was deleted and the Skyrocket, now powered solely by a rocket engine, was carried to altitude under a B-29 in the same way as the X-1. The man who flew it during this stage of its flight test programme was Bill Bridgeman, a former bomber pilot who, until he joined the Douglas Aircraft Company after a spell as a civil airline pilot, had never flown a jet aircraft. During the Skyrocket's early flights, in which Bridgeman pushed it to the border of the speed of sound, 'Chuck' Yeager often flew as chase pilot in an F-86 Sabre, and Bridgeman admitted that he found the presence of 'Mr Supersonic' a considerable comfort.

The Skyrocket went supersonic for the first time on 5 April 1951 and Bridgeman later gave a graphic account of the flight.

On the long path up I review the flight to assure myself that it is still securely locked in my mind, ready to be put into effect if this time I drop. The navigator's altimeter above my head reads 25,000 feet. In the draughty forward compartment of the bomber boring her way up through the fifty-degree below-zero sky the cold penetrates the cloth of the pressure suit that is tightly bound to my legs.

28,000 feet! Here's where I get off. I get to my feet and make my way to the Skyrocket's cramped cockpit. Performing the familiar tasks that set things in order I prepare the plane for the flight.

'Five minutes.' Change oxygen over to the Skyrocket's limited supply. Apply full pressure into the helmet. Instrumentation power switch on. I release the valve that pressurizes the cabin for 35,000 feet.

'Four minutes.' Here is where we can meet trouble if there is to be any. Turn rocket master switch to on. Pressurize rocket system. The rocket pressure gauges are all showing green. I am expectant and alert and the tension automatically increases, and now I am on edge.

'Fifty seconds.' In the twilight of the B-29's belly the black faces of the pressure gauges command my attention. The white, quivering needles are holding and I watch them intently. Then the white sliver on the middle gauge slips out of line! Number three system pressure is weakening, and as the needle drops I am suddenly drained. Again we must give up!

'No drop. This is a failure.' That's that. I yank the circuit breakers up, shut off the valve beside me that puts the rocket system back to sleep, and begin to secure the plane. As I do I hear, with disbelief, George starting his ten-second count-down as if he had not heard my order to cancel the flight.

'Ten, nine . . .' slowly he calls off the seconds. I shout through my throat mike, 'Don't drop me, George.' But the voice doesn't stop and the count continues in my ears as I frantically repeat, 'Aren't you receiving me? Don't drop me; the pressure on number three system has failed.' No response.

'. . . eight, seven,' the steady count moves on unperturbed. I can't break through. George has his thumb on the key. He does not hear my frantic protestings. Now, as I futilely shout into the helmet in the hope that he takes his thumb off the mike key between seconds, I work furiously to reinstate the ship for flight.

The hollow voice drones on, ticking off the seconds. 'Five . . . four . . .' And still I try to get through, to break the count. 'Don't drop.' There is no doubt. No getting out of it now. He is going to let me go.

Am I forgetting anything? God, am I forgetting anything? I force myself to retrace the steps I performed to inactivate the Skyrocket, although I know there is not enough time to do it thoroughly. There are some big decisions to be made in three seconds . . . whether or not to hit the first rocket switch and take a chance of her blowing all over the sky or whether to jettison the load of fuel that will allow me a longer chance at gliding home. To jettison the fuel is bad; if only one tank empties she will lose her balance. Make up your mind, quick!

'Three . . . two . . . one . . . drop!'

The bright light of the world bursts over my eyes as I plunge through the trap floor from the protective dark gut of the sheltering bomber – into the middle of the sky-sea without a lifebelt. It's a living, moving world, where the Skyrocket must be alive. She is dropping fast with her heavy load – 15,650 pounds of pure rocket, silent as a bird dropped by a hunter, straight down with no control of her own yet.

I reach for the first rocket switch! Six seconds pass before the explosion, before the rocket blasts with a giant reassertion. She lives! And hopefully and thankfully I click on the rest of the tubes as fast as possible. The force slams in . . . number two, *slam* . . . number three, *slam* . . . number four . . . she is accelerating with all the power in the world blasting her on. The rockets have lit, miraculously enough, but I don't expect them to last long with the pressure low in number three. But as long as they are burning I will follow the flight pattern.

And then I remember, as if they were people I left a long time ago, the crew. No more than thirty-five seconds have passed since George dropped me. It seems an enormously long time since I have opened my mouth to speak.

'Goddam it, George, I *told* you not to drop me.' The words are ridiculously inadequate and without purpose.

Pete Everest, another test pilot, laughs somewhere in the sky in his F-86, and his is the first voice I hear: 'You got keen friends, Bridgeman . . .'

I follow the plan that I have carried in my head these last three months. She is to pick up five-tenths of a Mach number, almost a third faster than she has ever demonstrated. Up to this minute I have crossed into the shallow end of the supersonic region and then backed out quickly. Now I am all the way in, and I will be here until the fuel burns up. I can barely read my altitude with the altimeter 100-foot hand a revolving blur obscuring the 1,000-foot and 10,000-foot hands.

The rocket-cylinder seconds are running out. Twenty seconds remain for the push over the top. I watch the fire-warning devices, and listen. If I detect the buzz of flutter on the controls I will immediately cut off the rockets.

We are at the top, 45,000 feet, or close to it. As she begins the long arc over the top I am lifted up from my seat and my body grows lighter by the second as I approach zero 'g'. All the black dials before me are shifting, changing, and whirling. I fly by only one now – the accelerometer that is measuring the degree of 'g' I am putting on the ship. The 'g' hand holds steady on .3, and briefly I move my eyes to the Mach-meter dial moving up to 1.2 . . . 1.25 . . . *What the hell is this?* She is rocking gently and rapidly back and forth like a cradle. A helpless feeling; my body, light as a balloon, oscillates from side to side with the ship. I grab the stick to dampen the gyration, but the ailerons have little effect.

Before fear has a chance to set in solidly the Skyrocket is in the sloping dive and steady once again. The Mach needle reaches towards 1.3 and I hang on and wait for the rockets to quit . . . 1.32 . . . 1.38 . . . 1.4 . . . *powie* . . . she decelerates in the brick wall as one rocket cuts off and *slam, slam, slam,* the other tubes follow, pulling me violently into the instrument panel. One by one I hear them splutter off as I lie jammed tight against the wall of the whirring dials, and then she is silent

146

and powerless once more, pointing her way across the sky, following the path she was directed along.

On the way home I am to pick up added data – side slips and constant-speed runs. Then a dead-stick landing on my return . . .

Three miles of runway behind her. She is rolling at twenty miles an hour to a stop and I open the canopy. The hot, clean desert air washes over my face and the white flash-bulb brightness of the lake bed bursts into my eyes. Now she is motionless. It is over. Everything is done; the chain of steps is completed. There is no emergency to anticipate, no race to keep the steps moving. It is finished. I have nothing to remember.

In the early 1950s the quest for higher speeds and greater altitudes gathered momentum. The original Bell X-1, which had taken man to a speed of over 1,000 mph, was retired to end its days on permanent display in the National Air Museum of the Smithsonian Institution, but three more aircraft – the X-1A, X-1B and X-1D – were built to carry on the research programme. The X-1D was destroyed in August 1951 when it was jettisoned from a Boeing B-50 carrier aircraft over Edwards AFB following an explosion, fortunately without any casualties, and much of the workload now devolved on the X-1A.

Although marred by a number of accidents and technical setbacks, the NACA piloted rocket programme did not result in loss of life until 1954, and the aircraft involved was another Bell design, the X-2. Unlike the X-1, the X-2 had swept wing and tail surfaces and was designed to reach speeds in the order of 2,000 mph. To counter the high temperatures that would be met at such speeds, stainless steel featured predominantly in the aircraft's construction. The X-2 was powered by a Curtiss XLR-25 rocket motor.

Two X-2s were built. Disaster overcame the first in May 1954, when an explosion ripped through it as its liquid oxygen tank was being topped up in the belly of the B-50 mother ship. The X-2 pilot and one B-50 crew member were killed, but quick action in jettisoning the rocket aircraft by the B-50 pilot prevented further casualties. The second X-2 made its first powered flight on 18 November 1955, piloted by Lieutenant-Colonel Frank Everest, but this aircraft was also destroyed in a fatal crash on 27 September 1956 after a flight in which the pilot, Captain Milburn Apt, was officially stated to have flown faster than any other human being.

At that time, the fastest recorded speed was 1,650 mph – Mach 2.5 – achieved by Charles Yeager in the Bell X-1A in December 1953. The launch, from a B-29 at 30,000 feet, was trouble-free and Yeager ignited three of his four rockets, taking the aircraft to 45,000 feet before levelling out and hitting the fourth rocket switch. On this flight the X-1A had 1,200 gallons of fuel, enough for four minutes under power. Yeager went supersonic while still in level flight at 45,000 feet, then he pulled back the stick and took the X-1A in a dizzying climb to 80,000 feet, exceeding Mach 1.8 on the way up. Levelling out again, he pushed all four rockets to full power for the last minute of the flight and watched the needle of the Machmeter creep up to 2.5, the aircraft shuddering and vibrating alarmingly. Then, without warning, the X-1A went out of control. Yeager described it later :

Suddenly the aircraft would not respond to me. It was out of control for about one minute, shooting down from 80,000 to almost 25,000 feet. I cut off the power immediately. I was not unconscious, but I was very scared. I wanted to survive. I was doing everything possible to make the plane fly again. I knew I could not get out; the plane had no ejection seat. If I had had time I would have prayed. I was subjected to high forces. My body was aching and my nerves were strained. I had no time to tell the others over the radio what had happened.

I worked like mad. I didn't want to die. Finally, down at 25,000 feet, I regained control of the plane. I went level and glided down slowly to the dry bed of Lake Muroc. The ground crew were there already. They helped me out of my pressure suit. I was sweating and felt exhausted. They took me to the base hospital, where I was X-rayed. Fortunately no bones were broken.

It was Yeager's last flight in the X-1A, for his tour of duty at Wright AFB was over. One of the pilots who took over from him was Joseph Walker, a highly experienced member of the NACA test team who, on 8 August 1955, almost came to grief when the liquid oxygen tank exploded as the X-1A was being prepared for a drop from its B-29 carrier. The time was 1342, just ninety seconds before the drop was due to take place.

Flying close alongside the B-29, in an F-86 chase plane, was Major Arthur Murray, who earlier had piloted the X-1A to a new record height of over 90,000 feet. Watching the rocket plane intently, he suddenly saw a small cloud of white vapour escape from its underside and, almost in the same instant, heard a noise like cannon shells bouncing along his aircraft – the shock wave of the explosion. He realized what had happened almost immediately, and strove to keep his voice calm and reassuring as he called up Walker, strapped in the X-1A's cockpit.

'Okay, Joe? Looks like an explosion. Doors peeled off outside. Are you okay?'

There was no reply.

'You look okay from outside,' Murray continued. 'Joe, are you all right? You, in the bomb bay, get in and take a look at him. It blew up in the wheel well.'

Two crew members, Jack Moise and Charles Littleton, scrambled down through the swirling white vapour into the bomb bay and saw at once that the Lox tank had been ruptured. They also saw that the shackles holding the X-1A to the B-29 were loose and that the aircraft might drop away at any moment. Despite the danger, both men set to work to free Joe Walker from the rocket plane's cockpit, balanced precariously with one foot on the B-29 and the other on top of the X-1A's fuselage. Their complete disregard for personal safety would later bring them the award of the NACA Distinguished Service Medal.

Walker, meanwhile, had been temporarily stunned by the

explosion. Now he recovered to find that the radio was completely dead. In a flash, his highly trained mind grasped what must have happened, and he knew that he had to get out quickly, before there were more explosions. Automatically, his fingers flicked over the switches, cutting off all power and expelling the air from the pressurized cockpit. It blasted out with a roar, and a few moments later Moise and Littleton raised the canopy and reached down into the cockpit to drag the pilot out.

Walker's problems were only just beginning, for in escaping from the X-1A's cockpit he had disconnected his oxygen line, and at 31,000 feet, without oxygen, his life would quickly be forfeit. Flopping like a stranded fish into the belly of the B-29, he scrambled up, pushing Littleton aside, and headed for the flight-deck, where he knew spare oxygen bottles were kept. The B-29 pilot, Stan Butchart, looked back and saw Walker staggering towards him, hampered by his pressure suit; he also saw the X-1A pilot's face. It was turning blue. Quickly, Butchart seized the nearest oxygen bottle and plugged Walker in. The latter took a few deep breaths, then smiled. He was safe now.

But the threat of the damaged X-1A still remained, and Butchart lost no time in checking with Major Murray over the R/T for the latest assessment. Murray reported that he had seen a short burst of flame spurting from the X-1A, but it had quickly disappeared and there seemed to be no immediate risk of fire. However, a lot of skin surrounding the rocket plane's engine bay had been blown clean away, together with the undercarriage doors. The force of the explosion had blown down the X-1A's main undercarriage, which now dangled in the slipstream. Later, Murray found that he had been very lucky; fragments of the X-1A had struck his F-86 as they whirled away, almost knocking off the cockpit canopy.

As Stan Butchart took the B-29 down in a cautious descent towards Muroc, his crew had time to make a more thorough appraisal of the damaged X-1A. Their one collective thought now was whether it might be possible to save the rocket plane, but the crew chief, Dick Payne, quickly confirmed that it would not be possible to land the B-29 with the X-1A's wheels in the 'down' position. Joe Walker climbed carefully back into the X-1A's cockpit to check on the position of the undercarriage lever, but it was in the 'up' position; there was nothing he could do to raise the wheels. Attempts to jettison the X-1A's substantial fuel load were also unsuccessful.

In the NACA operations room at Edwards AFB, Joseph Vensel, the X-1A project chief, had been following the drama. Now, realizing that nothing could be done to bring back the X-1A intact, he ordered Butchart to drop it. A few minutes later, after some difficulty – for the explosion had damaged the release mechanism – the rocket plane fell away from the B-29 and exploded in a great spout of flame on the desert floor. The B-29 crew and Joe Walker watched it go in silence. Then Arthur Murray's voice crackled over the R/T: 'I hate to see this,' he said. It was a sentiment they all echoed profoundly.

Another member of the NACA team who had followed the efforts to save the damaged X-1A from the operations room was a young test pilot named Scott Crossfield, who had also flown the Bell aircraft to more than 1,000 mph. Four years later, he was to become the first man to fly a new and far more advanced rocket research aircraft, designed to fill the gap between embryo rocket-powered research types and the space vehicles that would eventually place an American in orbit: the North American X-15A.

Following preliminary design studies by the NACA, together with a design competition that encompassed most of the US aircraft industry, North American Aviation was awarded, in December 1955, a contract for three prototypes of a manned research aircraft which was to have a design speed of at least Mach 7 and to be capable of reaching an altitude of at least 264,000 feet, or fifty miles above the earth. The powerplant was to be a Thiokol XLR-99-RM-1 rocket motor developing a thrust of 57,600 pounds, although initial flight tests with the first two X-15As were made with two Reaction Motors LR-11-RM-5s, each of 8,000-pound thrust, the larger engine not being ready. Because of the high friction that would be encountered at hypersonic speeds, the X-15's basic structural materials were titanium and stainless steel, the entire airframe being covered with an 'armoured skin' of nickel alloy steel designed to withstand temperatures of up to 550°C.

The first X-15A flew for the first time on 10 March 1959, carried under the starboard wing of a giant eight-engined B-52 Stratofortress 'mother' aircraft. It was not released on that occasion, the first free flight – without power – being made on 8 June, with Scott Crossfield at the controls. On 17 September, with Crossfield once again in the pilot's seat, the X-15A was launched on its first powered flight, dropping from a height of 38,000 feet. The rockets cut in 5,000 feet lower down and Crossfield took the aircraft in a shallow climb to Mach 2.3, about 1,500 mph. The fuel was exhausted four minutes after the launch and Crossfield came round in a turn to make a dead-stick landing on Lake Muroc, touching down at 150 mph. When ground crew inspected the X-15A, they found that alcohol from a broken fuel pump had flowed into the after engine bay and a savage and undetected fire had broken out, burning through a large area of aluminium tubing, fuel lines and valves. It was a sight which, Crossfield later admitted, made him 'sick with disappointment'. Nevertheless, repairs were carried out in twenty-three days and the aircraft was soon ready for its second powered flight.

A number of snags, usually associated with the fuel system, were encountered and had to be solved before the second flight could be made, but eventually, on 17 October 1959, Crossfield and the X-15 were launched from the B-52 at 41,000 feet over the desert. With all eight rocket tubes blazing, the X-15 quickly picked up speed and the pilot took it in a supersonic climb to 55,000 feet, where he levelled out and made some high-speed manoeuvres before climbing again to 67,000 feet, the maximum altitude for this flight. After the rockets burned out, Crossfield then took the X-15 in a supersonic glide at Mach 1.5, levelling out at 50,000 feet.

At that moment, as the X-15 'backed' through the sound barrier, Crossfield sensed rather than saw a sudden blur of light flash past his nose, dangerously close. It was Joe Walker, flying an F-104 chase plane. Startled and alarmed, Crossfield radioed:

'There goes my chase, right across my bow.' It had been a near miss – too near. Apart from that one incident, however, the remainder of the flight was uneventful and Crossfield made an excellent landing on the dry lake.

Five days later Crossfield was airborne in the X-15 once again, with plans to push the speed up to Mach 2.6 at an altitude of 85,000 feet. However, the flight had to be abandoned when the pilot detected a malfunction in his oxygen system, and bad weather delayed further testing until 5 November. This time, the weather was perfect and the pre-flight checks indicated no snags at all. It looked as though the stage was set for a perfect launch.

The count-down reached zero and the slender X-15 dropped sharply away from its pylon under the B-52's wing. Rapidly, Crossfield's gloved fingers flicked over the series of toggles that ignited the aircraft's rocket barrels. They lit up with a thud, and an instant later Crossfield was pressed into his seat by the acceleration as the X-15 began to surge forward under the tremendous power of its motor. Everything seemed to be functioning normally.

Then, without warning, a jarring explosion shook the aircraft. A quarter of a mile behind, test pilot Bob White, flying an F-104 chase plane, noticed a sudden red glare blossom out near the X-15's rocket exhaust. Anxiously, he radioed: 'Looks like you had an explosion in the rocket motor.' Then, a second later: 'You have a fire!'

In the X-15's cockpit, the fire warning light flashed on just as White's call came over the R/T. Like other rocket plane pilots before him, Crossfield felt a sudden chill of fear. The X-15 was loaded with nine tons of liquid oxygen and alcohol, and if the fire spread to the tanks the explosion would turn the aircraft and its pilot into a cloud of white-hot vapour.

Automatically, his reflexes acting with the speed born of years of experience in testing high-performance aircraft, Crossfield shut down the X-15's rocket motor. The aircraft's acceleration fell away, but now the tons of fuel that remained on board were beginning to drag it earthwards at frightening speed. A thick trail of white, frozen gas streamed out across the sky as Crossfield operated the fuel jettison mechanism. On the ground far below, there was a moment of near-panic among members of the X-15 team who had been watching the flight through powerful binoculars; some of them mistook the white gush of escaping fuel for an explosion ripping the aircraft apart.

Crossfield radioed that he intended to land on the nearest dry lake. The X-15, still 1,000 pounds heavier than normal, was plummeting down at more than 300 miles an hour, way above the normal glide speed on the approach to land. Bob White, following the rocket plane down in his F-104, called out the rapidly decreasing altitude. At 6,000 feet, Crossfield pointed the X-15 towards Rosamund Dry Lake and levelled out to begin his approach, intent on getting down as quickly as possible. He held the nose of the aircraft high to reduce speed and pressed the microphone button, cutting off any radio transmissions that might interfere with his concentration and distract him during the crucial stages of the landing.

The ground rushed past in a blur, terrifyingly fast. Seconds later, the X-15's landing skids hit the surface of the dry lake with a terrific crunch. The nose slammed down brutally and the aircraft ploughed across the desert floor, trailing a vast plume of dust in its wake. Then it slewed to a stop, so suddenly that Crossfield though the skids had collapsed. The noise died away and he sat there in the cockpit – the safest place in the X-15 in the event of a fire on the ground – and waited for the rescue helicopter to appear.

It was on the scene within two minutes. Ground crewmen climbed out and unfastened the X-15's canopy, helping Crossfield out of the cockpit. Together, they walked round the aircraft and surveyed the damage. It was heartbreaking. The X-15's rocket motor was a burnt-out shambles and the plane's back was broken. To Crossfield, it seemed as though some alien power was determined to thwart man's bid to reach space. Yet he had escaped with his life; it could so easily have been different.

After a two-month delay, the research programme resumed with the X-15A-1, which flew for the first time under power on 23 January 1960. Crossfield's damaged X-15A-2 was repaired and flying again early in February, and by October both aircraft had made over twenty successful flights. A third aircraft, the X-15A-3, had been made ready for flight in the summer of 1960, but it was seriously damaged on the ground on 8 June by an explosion in the propellant system, and it was several months before it could be made airworthy. This was not the end of the disasters: on 9 November 1962, X-15A-2 landed without flaps, collapsed its undercarriage and ended on its back, fortunately without serious injury to the pilot.

By this time the X-15s had chalked up a number of notable record flights. On 27 June 1962 Joe Walker, now chief test pilot for NASA (The National Aeronautics and Space Administration) reached a speed of 4,104 mph in the X-15A-1 after the engine burned for eighty-nine seconds instead of the normal eighty-four seconds, while on 17 July 1962 Major Bob White, USAF, climbed to a height of 59.6 miles in X-15A-3 and qualified for the award of his US Astronaut's 'Wings' by travelling more than fifty miles above the earth. Other pilots who subsequently qualified for a similar award while flying the X-15 were Lt Col. Rushworth and Captain J. Engle, USAF, Mr John McKay of NASA and Joe Walker, who on 22 August 1963 set a new record by reaching a height of 67.08 miles.

Following its accident in November 1962 the X-15A-2 was almost completely rebuilt and the aircraft was modified to withstand speeds of up to Mach 8. The aircraft flew in its new form on 28 June 1964, when Major Rushworth achieved a speed of 2,964 mph at 83,000 feet. On 18 November, 1966, the X-15A-2, now fitted with two drop tanks designed to improve the burning time from 83 to 150 seconds, reached a speed of 4,250 mph in level flight at an altitude of 100,000 feet, piloted by Major Pete Knight of the USAF.

That same year, 1966, NASA was saddened by the death of Joe Walker, who at that time was probably the world's most experienced supersonic research pilot. On 8 June he was flying an F-104 in close formation with a North American B-70 Valkyrie supersonic bomber prototype when the two aircraft collided. Both were destroyed; one of the two B-70 pilots baled out, but

Walker's F-104 exploded in flames and there was no hope of survival. For a man who had risked his life so often, and who had done so much to further man's knowledge of the unknown realms on the edge of space, it was a singularly futile way to die.

Yet death was never far away from any of them, whenever they flew, for no matter how perfectly everything checked out, you always had to expect the unexpected where rockets were concerned. One of the men who knew that better than most was 'Chuck' Yeager, who again came close to losing his life in 1963. Yeager, now a full Colonel, was one of the pilots responsible for testing the Lockheed NF-104A, a modified version of the basic F-104 with a rocket motor mounted under the fuselage. Three such aircraft belonged to the Aerospace Research Pilot School at Edwards AFB, and were used for training future astronauts in ballistic flight techniques.

The idea was that the NF-104A would accelerate in level flight until Mach 2.15 was reached under the power of its jet and rocket motors, then pull up into a zoom climb. The jet engine would be cut off as the aircraft passed through 80,000 feet and the NF-104A would be boosted up to heights of over 100,000 feet by the rocket. As it coasted 'over the top', the trainee-astronaut pilot would experience a state of weightlessness, during which he had to carry out a variety of tasks. When Yeager was testing one of these aircraft in December 1963, things went badly wrong and the NF-14A went into a flat spin at 101,000 feet. Nothing the pilot could do would bring it out, and Yeager, severely shaken, managed to eject successfully as the aircraft plunged back into the denser layers of the atmosphere.

By the late 1960s the X-15 was coming to the end of its useful life. One aircraft, the well-tried X-15A-2, had its entire airframe coated with a special ablative material similar to that used to coat the nose-cones of missiles. This material was designed to burn away progressively during hypersonic flight, enabling temperatures of up to 1,400°C to be withstood. In the newly-modified X-15A-2, Major William J. Knight of the USAF reached the highest speed ever attained in an X-15, 4,534 mph (Mach 6.72) on 3 October 1967.

The X-15 made its last flight on 24 October 1968, and soon afterwards the programme was suspended. The eyes of America were now on the Apollo lunar landing programme, and the tremendous achievement of the first manned moon landing in 1969 largely eclipsed the efforts of the X-15 team.

Yet the contribution made by the X-15 – and, indeed, by the rocket aircraft which had preceded it – to America's space programme was incalculable, particularly in the development of the space shuttle, designed to carry men and materials into earth orbit and to return to earth in the same way as a piloted aircraft. This is the forerunner of the commercial spacecraft of tomorrow, which one day will set the feet of mankind on the real road into the universe.

And in years to come, when the prototype space shuttles seem as antiquated as the Wright Flyer that started man's search for the conquest of the sky, perhaps future generations to whom space travel is routine might pause for a few moments to remember Yeager, Bridgeman, Joe Walker, Bob White, Crossfield and all the others who, because it was their chosen career, risked their lives to ride the rockets and make it possible.